Beginner's Guide to

Floorquilts

No-Sew

Fabric Decoupaged Floorcloths

Carolyn French

Copyright © 2013 by Carolyn French

All rights reserved. No part of this publication, covered by the copyright hereon, may be used in any form or reproduced by any means—graphic, electronic, or mechanical, which would include photocopying, scanning, information storage and retrieval systems, or otherwise, without written permission from the author/publisher. Any attempt to resell, share, or distribute this guide or variations is strictly prohibited by law. The designs in this guide may be used to make items for personal use only. Any constructed items made from the patterns can be sold, as long as they carry a conspicuous label with the following information: *Designs Copyright © 2013 by Carolyn French from "Beginner's Guide to Floorquilts."*

 Attention Teachers: You are encouraged to use to use this guide when teaching, and may photocopy pages as needed for this use.

Great care has been taken to ensure that the information in this guide is accurate, and presented in good faith. Having no control over the choices of materials or the procedures used, the author/publisher shall not have any liability to any person or entity with respect to any loss or damage, directly or indirectly, by the information contained in this guide. No warranty is provided, and no results are guaranteed. For your safety, please follow all instructions carefully, and contact the author if you have any questions or comments at: french66c@gmail.com or floorquilts.weebly.com

ISBN-13: 978-1478170266

ISBN-10: 1478170263

BISAC: Crafts & Hobbies/Quilts & Quilting

"Mischievous Puppies"

Cover Designer: *Nathan French*

Book Designer, Text, and Artwork: *Carolyn French*

Photography and Technical: *Nathan and Carolyn French*

Trademark (™) names, and registered trademark (®) names are used in this guide in name only (without the symbols) for the benefit of the reader and owner, with no intention of infringement. Although names could not always be found, every effort was made to give credit to the textile artists and/or producers of the beautiful fabrics featured in this guide.

Acknowledgments

I would like to express a very special thanks to my son, Nathan French, who made it possible for me to create this enlightening and engaging guide. His skill with the camera is to be admired, as well as his patience. He sacrificed much of his time to help me with the technical issues of this publication, and for that I am very grateful! I would also like to thank my other son, Daniel, and of course, my unselfish and loving husband, Dan. They have both been very tolerant and supportive of my floorquilting adventures. A special "thank you" goes out to all the textile artists who created the beautiful fabrics in this guide, making it possible for us to enjoy the wonderful craft of floorquilting!

CONTENTS

Floorquilts: Walkable Works of Fabric Art

When we think of quilts, we no longer just visualize the traditional patchwork quilt adorning a bed, or the contemporary art quilt enlivening a wall. Over the years, our favorite fabrics and quilt designs have also beautified and personalized our floors. The use of clear protective sealants makes it possible for us to walk on such fabrics without any worry of wear-n-tear. These durable, walkable works of fabric art are known as "floorquilts."

The techniques used to create these appealing floor coverings are very similar to fabric decoupage, patchwork quilting, and floorcloth painting, only you do not need to be a crafter, a quilter, or an artist to create one. **If you can cut with scissors, or stroke with a paintbrush, you can make a floorquilt.** The construction of a floorquilt mainly involves the piecing of treated fabric shapes onto a primed canvas to create an attractive design. Several coats of a *user-friendly* decoupage medium and a *water-based* finish are then applied to protect the fabrics and enhance the colors—thus the name—fabric decoupaged floorcloths. Much of this guide is centered on these floorquilting fundamentals. Whether you are a younger person who has never sewn, or an older person with years of quilting experience, a novice or an artist, you will soon discover that no-sew floorquilts are easy and enjoyable to make.

The pages ahead will guide you step-by-step through simple hands-on instructions for making a variety of appealing floorquilts and *off-the-floor* items. Each project will progressively build on your previous skills, while stirring your creativity. No project is more difficult than another, but some will require more steps and/or materials. The traditional and contemporary designs range from geometric and floral, to whimsical and pictorial. Each was chosen so as to spark your imagination, and inspire you to devise something new and different; stepping outside of your comfort zone as you boldly create any design that you can think up. After-all, there is more fun and satisfaction when we make something that is of our own distinct voice and individuality. Before you begin, read through the valuable discussions on design, fabrics, and canvas. Take some time to read these thoroughly, and don't forget to check out *A Few Traditional Quilting Patterns* and *Using Stained Glass Patterns* for additional design ideas and inspiration. More importantly, don't forget to have fun!

With each floorquilt you make, you will have a personal and walkable work of fabric art that will last for many years to come....

Getting Started

Although no special skills are needed to make a floorquilt, you will need to have patience, be accurate, and have a little sense of humor should a problem occur. Pages 74 and 75 contain six common problems and solutions that I would advise you look over before you begin. Take some time to get all the right materials, and follow the techniques as described, studying them (on pages 12–28) until you're familiar with each. Before you choose your first project, be sure to also read *Designing Your Floorquilt* on page 10.

The techniques in this guide can be used to create a floorquilt from any design of your choosing and creativity.

Floorquilts are durable because of the number of protective coatings—three coatings of a matte decoupage medium and three coatings of a *water-based* polycrylic or *water-based* polyurethane satin finish. These non-toxic and user-friendly finishes will not only protect the fabrics, they will also enhance the colors and prints. What is especially nice is that any spills can easily be wiped clean.

Fabric decoupaged floorcloths are ideal for people with pets or allergies, and for those who have simply run out of places to showcase their favorite fabrics and quilt designs. They look great under doorways, sinks, and appliances, at bedsides, and in dining, office, sewing, and hobby areas—anywhere there is a hard "flat" surface, such as hardwood, linoleum, cement, and close-fitting tile. Floorquilts should not be placed outside. They can, though, be used under a covered porch that is protected from the elements. These wipe-able floor coverings are spill-proof, but not entirely waterproof. Any spills should be removed as they occur (see page 29, under "Floorquilt Care & Handling").

▶Note: For information and web addresses on unit conversions, please refer to page 94 of this guide.

The list of materials that follows (on pages 7 and 8) **is for a 24" x 36" or similar size floorquilt.** You can, of course, make your floorquilt any size that you like. Just make sure to compensate for the amount of materials before you start. **Lastly, take your time and enjoy the experience!**

Tools & Materials

Most tools and materials can be found at local hobby, craft, fabric, and hardware stores, and craft, fabric, and hardware departments at local department stores. Sources are found on pages 92 and 93.

■ Artist canvas—very heavy-weight 12 ounce cotton duck, around 26" x 38", or 12 ounce (or heavier) pre-primed floorcloth canvas—24" x 36" (see pages 16 and 17, and sources on page 92)

■ White acrylic gesso primer (not necessary with primed canvas—inexpensive brands will work well)

■ 100% cotton fabrics—½ yard for borders and 1 yard or more (made up of assorted fabrics) for central design (see *Selecting & Preparing Fabrics* on page 12)

■ Matte decoupage medium—Two 16 ounce containers (*Mod Podge* by Plaid)

■ Lint-free rag, such as an old hand towel or white cotton sock (for pressing decoupaged fabric)

■ Two smooth lint-free light-colored cloths (cotton/polyester for ironing fabrics, see page 14—step 7)

■ Water-based polycrylic (a combination of polyurethane and acrylic by *Minwax*) or water-based polyurethane protective finish (I prefer *Rust-Oleum Ultimate*) 8 ounce can of clear satin, found in most paint departments (see *A Word about Water-Based Finishes* on page 28) **Note:** Although very durable and flexible, some water-based polyurethanes have an ever slight amber hue, so they are not recommended for use over white fabrics. (I use *Minwax Polycrylic* over white fabrics, and *Rust-Oleum Ultimate* over everything else.)

■ Extra fine 220-280 grit sandpaper

■ Clear paste wax, such as *SC Johnson* or *Minwax,* found in floor care sections at most hardware stores

■ Thin plastic drop cloth (inexpensive), around 9 feet by 12 feet (will be divided into three sections)

■ Two inexpensive sponge brushes, and one stiff synthetic paintbrush (A synthetic brush is not necessary if purchasing canvas that is primed on both sides, as it is used to apply the primer.) A four-inch foam roller brush (for ultra-smooth surfaces) will prevent brush strokes in the decoupage medium, and is recommended for the second and third coats (see page 26—step 4).

■ Yardstick (a heavy plastic gridded ruler, 6" x 24", often called a quilt ruler, is helpful and optional)

■ 2" x 12" ruler and/or 2" x 18" gridded ruler used for drawing

■ Scissors—one pair of utility for cutting canvas and templates, and one pair of inexpensive fabric scissors

- Rotary and circle cutters are optional, but nice for cutting straight lines and accurate circles

- Self-healing cutting mat, ruled with a grid of one-inch squares (the larger–the better)

- Transparent plastic template sheets, found in quilting sections at fabric and hobby stores (see page 11)

- Pencils and sharpener to mark fabrics—silver, yellow, and orange pencils work well

- Graph paper (any size grid) for creating your own designs (see *Designing Your Floorquilt* on page 10)

- Math compass for marking accurate circles and curves

- Dark permanent marker for marking templates only

- Steam iron and ironing surface

- Non-skid rug backing compound or flat rubbery pad to prevent sliding and slipping

Optional, but Helpful Tools & Supplies

- Non-skid additive, such as *Skid-Tex*, can be added to the final coat of water-based finish to add texture (see page 27—step 5)

- Craft knife for cutting the inner sides of letters and smaller pieces

- Pattern cutting board—a large 36" x 60" inexpensive fold-out corrugated cardboard, printed with a 1" grid; convenient for marking long border strips, and larger geometric shapes (stores well)

- Triangle marking template—useful for marking and cutting many triangles, decreasing preparation time

- Quilt design stencils and multi-circle templates

- 6" square ruler to measure and cut square pieces more accurately and quickly

- Quilt and art quilt books and magazines for additional design ideas and inspiration

- Box, tub, and/or tote bag for supplies

Caution! Keep Your Work Area Protected & Safe

Try to work in a well-lit area that is free of lint, dust, pet hair, and other floating debris, particularly when you are applying the protective coatings. The debris can get stuck in the wet and drying finish, and is difficult to remove. Always protect your work area with a drop cloth. It is inexpensive, and goes a long way in protecting furniture and floors. Most important, never let children or anyone unfamiliar with the proper use of sharp objects, such as scissors and rotary cutters, in your work area unsupervised. The blades on a rotary cutter are razor sharp, so always cover the blade with its guard whenever it is not in use. When using a rotary cutter, watch your fingers, and cut along your ruler and away from yourself.

Quilting Techniques

Patchwork and appliqué are two of the most popular quilting techniques. The difference between the two is that in patchwork, small pieces of fabric are joined together, often in geometric shapes, in a set order, to form a design. Creating patchwork is called piecing. In appliqué, small pieces of fabric are cut into shapes, such as flowers, leaves, and butterflies, which are then applied to the surface of another larger fabric. Appliqué is an attractive complement to pieced work. Floorquilting combines both of these popular quilting techniques.

Be as accurate as possible when measuring, marking, and cutting your pieces. This will improve the over-all appearance of your finished floorquilt. Yes, it is true: you must "measure twice, and cut once."

It's Nice to Know!

"What's in a Block?"

The patchwork block is a single design unit repeated over the surface of a quilt. A block may be any size, and contain any number of pieces. Most patchwork blocks can be divided into a grid of equal-sized squares. A four patch block, for example, contains four equal-sized squares, and a nine patch contains—you guessed it—nine equal-sized squares. A single block quilt is a design in which one large block makes up the entire top. There are two basic block designs: **straight**—the sides of the blocks run parallel to the sides of the quilt, and **diagonal**—the blocks are set on point, with the sides of the blocks running diagonally to the sides of the quilt. Before planning your design, take a look at the traditional patchwork block patterns found on pages 85–89. These are but a few of the endless variety of designs that make up the patchwork block.

Designing Your Floorquilt

A reason why floorquilting is so enjoyable is that you can design your own projects. There are no absolute rules to designing floorquilts—your imagination is the limit. Whether a simple and traditional combination of squares, or an expressive arrangement of assorted shapes, there are many design possibilities, and none are too difficult to attempt. The designs in this guide are only suggestions, and nearly everything can be used as a design idea once you have learned to handle simple pieces. You may first want to start with a basic project, such as "Summer Bloom" on page 30. This is a beginner's project, using simple shapes, that I will walk you through step-by-step.

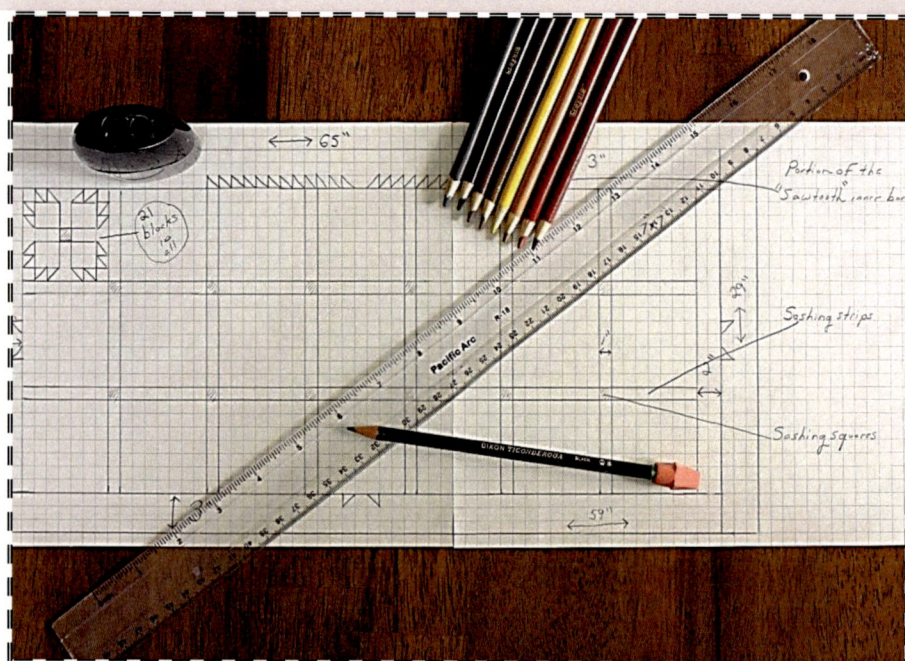

I have used graph paper to design every project in this guide. Each equal-sized square on your graph paper may allow for one inch on your floorquilt. Most patchwork block patterns, such as those on pages 85–88, can be drafted onto this type of paper. One latter design on page 48 will require specialized graph paper, ruled in hexagons.

For starters, you will want to outline a three-inch wide border on your graph paper. Use a lead pencil to mark a 24" x 36" rectangle (24 x 36 squares), next mark an 18" x 30" rectangle (18 x 30 squares). You now have a three-inch wide border. Before you design your first floorquilt, read *What's in a Block?* on page 9 and *Central Design* on page 19. **Pay close attention to color when designing your floorquilt, and think seriously of color arrangement in relation to the room your floorquilt will occupy.** An artist set of colored pencils with a variety of colors can better help you plan your design.

With graph paper and a pencil, you can easily customize the geometric patterns and designs featured in this guide to your own requirements and preference.

Sources of Inspiration

Your designs may start with those in this guide, but eventually you will want to consult a variety of other sources, such as quilting and design books. The best source of inspiration, however, comes from you. The things we see each day, whether a colorful bird in a garden, a playful and beloved pet, or a child's cherished toy; the feelings these create inside of us are often what inspire, and enable us to be so creative.

A Word about Templates

After you have created your design, you will want to make templates. Templates are firm patterns that you can mark around to transfer shapes onto fabrics. Template patterns for some of the projects in this guide are found on pages 76–84. Transparent vinyl or plastic template sheets are generally sold at hobby, craft, and fabric stores in the quilting sections (see page 93 for sources). Most precut shapes, such as squares, triangles, diamonds, circles, hexagons, and hearts, can also be purchased. After you have made the suggested templates for your chosen project, label each side—right or wrong. This is important, especially when you are working with uneven shapes. When you trace uneven shapes onto the wrong side of your fabric, you will want to turn your template to the wrong side (*right side down*). This will ensure that a leaf, for example, is not facing the left when it should have been facing the right. Additional information for constructing templates can be found under *Template Shapes* on page 31.

Accuracy is the Secret to Successful Floorquilting.

Selecting & Preparing Fabrics

One of the most delightful tasks in floorquilting is choosing the fabrics. Just about any color and print can be found—from floral, geometric, and abstract prints, to conversational, folkloric, and scenic. When selecting your fabrics, choose those with colors that you enjoy working with, and that will harmonize with the room your floorquilt will occupy. Have in mind the colors and prints that you want, and try not to stray from your color scheme, even if you should change the print or design.

When selecting your fabrics, search for those that are 100% cotton, or that have a higher ratio of cotton. Choose fabrics that are smooth and non-textured with a firm weave. Avoid any that are loosely woven, stretchy, or that ravel easily. Quilting-weight cotton fabrics will give the best results. See *How Much to Buy?* on page 15 before purchasing your fabrics.

Preparation

To give your fabrics a paper-like quality that is less prone to raveling, you will need to prepare them with a diluted mixture of decoupage medium. After your fabrics are treated, they will still retain the look of fabric, but will gain the more workable features of paper.

Apply an even coat of diluted decoupage medium to the right side of the fabric.

How To

1. With a steam iron, set to cotton, iron out any deep wrinkles or creases in your fabrics before you treat them.

2. Spread two plastic drop cloths—one over your work area, and one over a large flat well-ventilated area. The latter area is where you will place your treated fabrics to dry.

3. Pour the decoupage medium into a measuring cup until the cup is ¾ full. Add water until it reaches the one-cup line. Carefully mix the two together—¼ cup of water and ¾ cup of decoupage medium. This mixture will cover around two yards of fabric (one yard is around 36" x 45"). You can store the mixture in a plastic lidded container. I store my diluted mixture, which last for a few weeks, in an empty *Mod Podge* container, marked *diluted* on the lid. Continue with steps 4–8 on page 14.

4. Spread your fabrics, right side up, on the drop cloth. You can pin the fabrics to a flat piece of thick cardboard, placed underneath the drop cloth, to prevent them from sliding.

5. Using the sponge brush, apply the diluted decoupage medium to the *right side* of the fabrics—one piece at a time. Working from one side to the other, apply an even coat, making sure not to miss any areas (see photo on page 13). Do not worry about the cloudy color—the medium will dry clear.

6. Move the treated fabrics to the other drop cloth, keeping each as flat and smooth as possible. Pull the drop cloth straight around the edges to avoid any ripples or creases. It is normal to find that some decoupage medium has seeped through the fabrics. Lift the fabrics once while they are drying, and reposition them to speed the drying process and avoid creasing. If the humidity is high, run a small fan to help reduce the drying time. Keep any lines, such as stripes, straight as possible.

7. Once the fabrics are thoroughly dry, use a hot steam iron (set on cotton), and press them between two smooth light-colored lint-free pressing cloths to remove minor wrinkles and ripples. The pressing cloths will protect the treated fabrics, the iron, and the ironing surface. I like to use old (cotton/polyester) pillow cases.

8. You can now mark and cut your treated fabrics into the desired shapes required by your chosen project. First, if you have not already, read the chapter *Designing Your Floorquilt.* To avoid folds and creases, keep your treated fabrics flat or rolled (see *Storing Treated Fabrics* on page 16).

"Once the fabrics are thoroughly dry, use a steam iron (set on cotton), and press them between two smooth light-colored lint-free pressing cloths to remove minor wrinkles and creases."

How Much to Buy?

One yard of fabric measures around 36" x 45". Fat quarters or quilter's quarters are around 18" x 22", and can be inexpensively purchased pre-cut at most fabric stores. Fabrics are cut into yards, half yards, quarter yards, and eighths. Each floorquilt project in this book will require ½ yard of fabric for the borders, and an additional ½–1 yard (often made up of assorted fabrics) for the central design. Every project will list the sizes and variety of fabrics needed. Many online stores carry a wider variety of fabrics with prints and colors that cannot be found at your local stores. Simply type *fabric* on your search engine, and only shop at reputable stores. 100% cotton fabrics, with a smooth firm weave, work best (quilting-weight is preferred). ▶*Note*: *To convert inches to centimeters, please refer to page 94 of this guide.*

"I'm not greedy—I'm just materialistic!"

Cleanup

After you finish treating the fabrics, use an old bucket or plastic container, filled with warm water, to rinse your hands, the decoupage medium container, and the brush. If possible, rinse the container outside, as this will prevent any glue from getting on or in your sink, and possibly hardening in the drain. Gently squeeze the sponge brush dry to keep it in good condition. I wipe the excess medium off of everything with a paper towel before I rinse. I also allow the excess medium (*full-strength*) to dry in its plastic container. I pull the thin dried layer out of the container, and drop it in the trash the next day. Decoupage medium is very similar to white glue, and is user-friendly and environmentally safe.

Idea!

To prevent darker colors and prints from showing through lighter colors, decoupage an inexpensive sheet of muslin, or a similar colored fabric, to the wrong side of the lighter fabric. Once dried, treat this sheet as one piece of fabric, ironing and storing it like the others. Muslin is a thin cotton fabric that can easily be found, bleached or unbleached, at most fabric and hobby stores.

Storing Treated Fabrics

To avoid permanent creases, never fold your treated fabrics. Always store them flat or rolled. You can roll your fabrics around cardboard tubes, such as wrapping paper tubes or discarded paper towel and aluminum foil rolls. Smaller strips of fabric can be rolled without tubes, and scrap remnants may be stored in clear storage bags. I use clear freezer storage bags, which can be marked and stored flat, using a minimum amount of space. Masking tape will hold rolled fabrics in place, while preventing creases or wrinkles. The smallest bits of scraps are worth saving, and are used in a variety of projects—from a tiny leaf or flower on a placemat, to the narrow trim around a bookmark or coaster.

What is Canvas?

Canvas is an extremely heavy-duty fabric used for making tarps, tents, furniture, shoes, and other items for which strength and sturdiness are required. Due to its durability, canvas is also used as popular painting surfaces by artists the world over. Linen canvas and the less expensive cotton duck have become the preferred medium. Cotton duck is available in a variety of weights. A numbering system is used to describe the various weights and thickness, however, as the weight of the cloth goes up, the number goes down. These numbers may vary from seller to seller, so when purchasing your canvas, look for the weight—not the number. *Do not choose a canvas that has a weight less than 12 ounces.* 12 ounce unprimed (or primed, on one side or both) cotton duck canvas is heavy enough to lay flat on a floor after it is prepared without the edges rippling or curling. Unless it is very heavyweight, such as floorcloth canvas, avoid canvas that is commercially primed on both sides (page 17). *Sources for canvas are found on page 92.*

Selecting & Preparing the Canvas

The selection and preparation of your canvas is important. It is the backing, the base, the bones of your floorquilt. With this in mind, it is best to purchase heavy-weight 12-ounce (or heavier) 100% cotton duck. If not already primed, the canvas will need to be prepared with white acrylic gesso before applying your treated fabrics. Priming gives the cloth more stability, texture, and durability. Primed and raw canvas can both be purchased as blankets or rolls at your local craft or fabric store. Raw artist canvas (which I use) is less expensive, but it will need to be primed on both sides. If it's folded, it will also have creases. The primer does not have to be high quality. If you want a pre-primed canvas (eliminating preparation steps 1–4), choose only a heavy-weight 12-ounce canvas that will lie flat on the floor, such as floorcloth canvas. This canvas often has two coats of primer on one side, and one coat on the other. Piece your treated fabrics on the side that has only one coat. That side is more porous and textured, allowing for better adhesion and absorption of excess moisture. Canvas that is primed on just one side will need primer on the raw side. If you purchase such a canvas, use the side that "you" primed.

Be as accurate as possible when measuring, marking, and cutting the canvas.

Preparation

Apply acrylic primer to the raw sides of the canvas.

Primed canvas–skip to step 5
Primed on one side–ignore step 2

1. Measure and cut a 26" x 38" rectangle (for a 24" x 36" canvas), or what is according to your project. **Note**: Raw canvas will shrink around two inches after it is primed.

2. If you purchased raw (folded) canvas, you may need to iron out any folds or creases with a *steam* iron, set on cotton and steam. Some creasing may still be noticeable, but these will minimize as the quilt is constructed. Depending on your design, creases may be desirable, for they add to the character of a true patchwork quilt. Do not worry about stains from the steam, as they will be covered with primer.

3. Using a stiff paint brush, apply an even layer of gesso to the raw side of your canvas. Let dry. The canvas will shrink as it is drying. (If both sides of your canvas are now primed, proceed to step five.)

4. Turn your dried canvas over, and apply gesso to the other raw side. The canvas will shrink one-to-two inches while it is drying. Depending on the humidity, this could take from three to twelve hours.

5. If not the correct size, measure a 24" x 36" rectangle, or what is according to your project. (By taping together two large poster boards, I was able to construct a 24" x 36" template for accuracy.) Trim your canvas with utility scissors to the desired size. Snip off any loose fibers, and lightly sand any bumps.

6. For a three-inch wide border, place a mark three inches from every corner of the canvas. Using a yardstick, lightly pencil the border from one mark-to-another (see photo on page 17).

7. Minimize any large ripples and flatten any curled edges of primed canvas by ironing them between two pressing cloths, lifting the iron every few seconds. Do not allow the dried gesso to get too hot. Most ripples will minimize as your floorquilt is constructed. You are now ready to apply your central design.

A Word about Floorcloths

Floorcloths have been beautifying and personalizing floors for hundreds of years. Why, even George Washington owned a floorcloth. These functional floor coverings were also known as painted carpets, crumb cloths, summer floor mats, and many other names. Floorcloths were often made from the canvas of old recycled sails, and were used in place of expensive rugs to decorate entryways, hallways, parlors, and dining areas. Painted either by hand or by using stencils, their durable and washable finishes made them desirable additions to the home. The earliest cloth decorations consisted of geometric patterns featuring diamonds, cubes, squares, and checkers, imitating the fine flooring found in fashionable homes. Quilt patterns also became popular. Floorcloths eventually lost their popularity with the invention of linoleum, however, with the renewed interest in historic restoration, floorcloths made a comeback. They have been growing in popularity ever since.

Central Design & Borders

Central Design

The central design is everything within a floorquilt's borders. There are no absolute rules when it comes to planning your central design, other than it should have balance, and look right in its surroundings. For information on creating your design, see "Designing your Floorquilt" on page 10. When assembling the central design, lay out all your cut blocks and shapes in the order you would piece them onto your canvas. Check for color arrangement, placement, and alignment. You can keep track of each shape with small bits of marked masking tape. For example, "1a" could start the first block in the top row, "1b" the second, and "1c" the third. "2a" could start the second row, and so on. This is especially helpful if you need to reassemble your pieces at a later time, or if you are working with more complex patterns. The central design, or portions of it, will usually be decoupaged onto the canvas before the borders are applied. First, though, make sure to read the last two sections on page 75, which contains tips for applying the sealants.

Idea! Before marking and cutting your fabric shapes, you can use construction paper or photocopies of fabrics to make a preliminary design. You may rearrange, add, or leave out any pieces.
Remember, you are the artist!

Borders not only surround the central design, they also enhance the beauty of a floorquilt while uniting the design. When selecting a fabric for your border, choose one that repeats a color used in your central design. Whatever colors you choose, make sure that your border has a supporting role to the central design. It should not be too distracting, and it should unify your floorquilt. A border can be a single strip of fabric or multiple strips. It can be pieced or appliquéd (page 24), and the corners can be either straight or mitered— whatever you desire.

Construction & Application of Borders

1. An important first step in creating your borders is to take accurate measurements. Using a yard stick or a heavy plastic ruler (a gridded mat is also helpful), measure and mark, on the wrong side of your fabric, four border strips to the required measurements for your chosen project. The strips for the two longer sides will be the same length as the canvas sides. The strips for the shorter sides will be 2" longer. Pay close attention to the printed pattern, and mark with a sharpened white, yellow, orange, or silver pencil.

2. Lay your fabric on a large flat surface, or a self-healing mat if you are using a rotary cutter. Carefully cut the marked lines—one border at a time. If you are using a rotary cutter, align your ruler with the vertical grid line on the mat, and cut along the ruler and away from yourself, keeping your ruler aligned with your tracings.

3. Before adhering your border strips, first position them along each side of the canvas, checking for alignment and accuracy. If everything measures up, turn each strip wrong-side up. Mark the top of each strip to help you remember which direction to flip the border back over when you're finished applying the decoupage medium.

4. Pour some *full-strength* decoupage medium (around ¼ cup) into a small plastic lidded container. Using your sponge brush, apply an even *generous* coat of decoupage medium to the exposed canvas on one of the longer sides—the area where your long border strip will be placed (*see right photo*). In addition, apply the medium to the back edge (lengthwise) of the strip that will slightly overlap the central design. This will ensure better adhesion along the inner edge.

5. Turn your border strip over, and position into place. Check for proper alignment, allowing for one inch of overlapping fabric along the outer edge. Using a small old rag, rub the entire strip with short back-and-forth motions to adhere the strip, and to remove tiny air pockets. **Take your time to smooth out "all" air bubbles, no matter how small.** This is a crucial step in floorquilt construction.

The long "bottom" border strip in the photo above has been adhered to the decoupaged canvas, and is just slightly overlapping the edges of the central design. Notice the one-inch of overlapping fabric along the outer edge of the canvas. The overlap will be folded and decoupaged onto the back of the canvas.

6. Follow steps four and five for the other long border strip, then continue with step 7 on page 22.

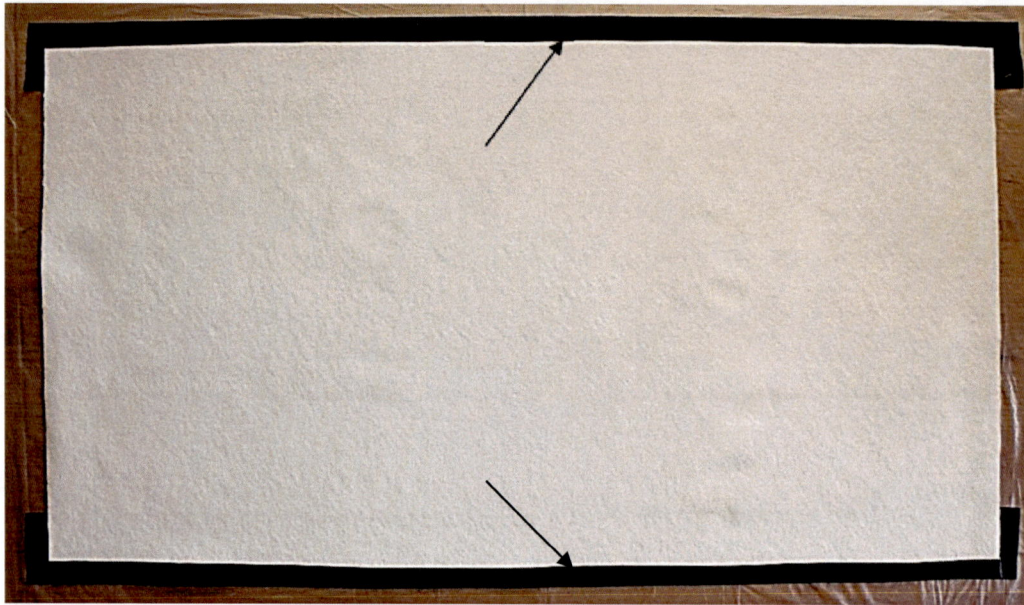

7. Once both of the long border strips are adhered to the front of the canvas, carefully turn your floorquilt over, and apply the decoupage medium to the wrong side of one of the strip's overlapping edge.

The one-inch border overlaps in the above photo are ready to be decoupaged onto the canvas backing.

8. Fold and press the overlap onto the back of the canvas. Rub the strip with an old rag, using short back-and-forth motions until it is *well-adhered*. Repeat this process with the other strip.

9. After the strips have dried, snip off any excess folded fabric at the corners with your utility scissors, as shown in the photo to the right.

10. Turn your floorquilt back over (right side up), and using the last two shorter strips, repeat steps 4 and 5 (page 21) on the shorter sides of the canvas. This time you will also apply the decoupage medium over the fabric of the longer strips, at the corners where the borders will overlap (see top photo on page 23).

The corners can be cut to appear mitered, where the two strips overlap. Just place your ruler diagonally from the corner edge, and cut the top strip overlap by a 45% angle (see the top of page 47).

When you apply the shorter border strips, first brush an even, "generous" amount of full-strength decoupage medium onto the canvas and over the fabric of the longer strips, where the strips will overlap at the corners, as shown in the left photo (step 10).

11. Turn your floorquilt onto its backside, and decoupage the wrong sides of the two shorter strip overlaps, folding them onto the back of the canvas, and pressing them with your rag, using short back-and-forth motions until *well-adhered*.

12. Slightly trim any folded corner flaps as needed (do not cut them off), so that when they are decoupaged and folded onto the canvas backing, they will be the same width as the other adhered edges—around one inch.

13. Decoupage the flaps and finger-press the folds at each corner into place, as shown below. Attach a spring-type clothespin onto the folds if necessary, and allow to *thoroughly* dry.

With a few exceptions, the borders will usually be applied "after" you have pieced your central design. The borders will help cover any minor irregularities and unevenness on all sides of the central design.

Inner & Pieced Borders

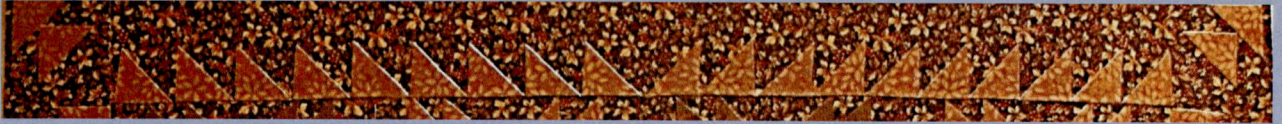

A narrow inner border, decoupaged onto the wider border, can help unify the colors and shapes in your design, and cover minor flaws along the central design edges. Borders that have been constructed from the repetition of shapes, such as the triangles above, are called pieced borders. The shapes usually repeat one that has been used in the central design (see *Bear's Paw,* page 34). They are often used as decorative inner borders, or as a row running through the center of the border strips, giving the appearance of a triple border.

Corner Blocks & Sashing Strips

Corner blocks are design elements that can help harmonize your over-all design. They can also solve problems by covering uneven overlaps and border prints that just do not turn the corner like you imagined. You will find simple instructions for constructing and applying a variety of corner blocks in many of the projects in this guide. The above corner block can be found on page 66. **Sashing or lattice strips** are the fabrics that separate blocks or squares, framing them while creating a latticework effect (see examples on pages 38, 44, and 64). There are two kinds of sashing: (1) continuous—one strip of fabric runs the full straight or diagonal length of the quilt, and (2) short sashing—the length of each strip equals the width of one block. You can add further interest to your floorquilt with the use of **sashing squares**—small simple squares, cut the same width as the sashing strips, and placed at the corners of each block (see bottom of page 38). Information on patchwork blocks can be found on page 9.

....*Cleanup*

Always keep a container of warm soapy water, and a clean rag or old hand towel close by when working with the decoupage medium. This will prevent the glue from drying on your fingers, and flaking onto your work in progress

Applying Protective Coatings

The key to making a floorquilt walkable and durable are several layers of protective coatings—three layers of a decoupage medium and three layers of a water-based polycrylic (polyurethane and acrylic) or polyurethane finish. A thin coat of wax will nourish the protective coatings, and aid in the resistance of abrasion, scuffing, and common household spills. Optional non-skid materials can be applied to both the surface and backing of your floorquilt to make it extra safe and non-slippery. Before applying the protective coatings, it is beneficial to read the last section under "Problem Solving" on page 75, which contains tips on how to apply the finishing coats.

Note: *While they are very durable and flexible, some water-based polyurethanes have an ever slight amber hue, so they are not recommended for use over bright white fabrics (see box on page 28).*

Idea! Roll a lint roller over your floorquilt to remove unnoticed lint, hair, and other floating debris before you apply the decoupage medium or water-based finish.

Applying the Decoupage Medium

1. Place your floorquilt on a new drop cloth in a well-lit and clean work area. Have a clean sponge brush and *full-strength* decoupage medium close-by, and on the drop cloth. Pour around ½ cup of the medium into a plastic lidded container.

2. With your sponge brush, apply an even coat of *full-strength* decoupage medium onto the *entire* surface of the floorquilt. Start with one corner of the quilt (the border) and work your way to the other—square-by-square—shape-by-shape. Press down any raised fabric, or bubbles underneath the fabric with your brush and fingers as you move along.

3. Once the entire surface is covered with decoupage medium, run a paper towel or napkin under the border perimeters of your floorquilt to remove any residue. I also wipe excess residue off the drop cloth, so it does not smear onto the back edges of the floorquilt.

4. After your floorquilt has dried (usually around three hours), apply two more *smooth* even coats of full-strength decoupage medium for a total of three coats—permitting each coat to *thoroughly* dry. To avoid brush strokes, apply the second and third coat with a smooth four-inch foam roller brush (*for extra smooth surfaces*). Roll over any air bubbles until they disappear. **Allow your floorquilt to dry for 24 hours before applying the water-based finish.**

5. Turn your floorquilt over, and brush some full-strength decoupage medium over the adhered border strip edges on the back, as shown in the picture below. After the medium has dried, apply one more coat. Allow the medium to spread over the edges, but not onto the floorquilt surface. Let dry.

Applying the Polycrylic or Polyurethane Finish

1. Gently stir the can of water-based finish with a paint stirrer before applying. Do not shake the can, as this will cause air bubbles within the finish.

To avoid bubbles, streaks, or debris in the water-based finish, make sure your brush is clean, and has an ample amount of finish. Brush steadily in one direction, and avoid over-brushing.

2. Apply an even (not heavy) coat of water-based finish with a new foam brush. A synthetic bristle brush can also be used. Make sure that your brush is well-loaded, and brush steadily in one direction. Avoid over-brushing, skipping, or brushing too fast, as this can cause excess bubbles and streaks in the finish.

3. After the finish is completely dry, lightly sand the coating with 220-280 grit fine sand paper. Depending on the humidity, the drying time could take anywhere from six-to-twelve hours. (If using a polycrylic finish, I recommend waiting a full 24 hours before applying the second coat.) Remove dust with a damp cloth when you are finished sanding. Sanding will smooth out rough spots and bubbles, and help the wet finish adhere to the previous coat.

4. Apply the second coat, repeating steps 1 through 3.

5. Repeat steps 1 and 2 for the final third coat. A fourth coat may be added if you will be placing your floorquilt in a high traffic area. **You may add an optional non-skid additive to the final coat to help prevent slipping** (sources on page 92). Follow the manufacturer's instructions—around one tablespoon is mixed with the final coat. Continue with steps 6 and 7 on page 28.

6. Once the final coat has completely dried, apply an even coat of water-based finish over the entire *backside* of the floorquilt. You can skip this step if you are applying a coat of non-skid backing, such as *Saf-T-Bak* (see sources on page 93). Allow the finish or backing to dry for 24 hours. Instead of applying a coat of non-skid backing, **you can choose to use a thin *smooth* non-skid rug pad**, which will prevent movement of the quilt and add comfort. Make sure your floor is free of dust, and is very clean before positioning the rug pad upon it. The pad will also minimize impressions from tile grooves and linoleum.

7. With a small clean cloth, wipe a thin coat of paste wax over the entire surface of the floorquilt. Allow the wax to dry. Gently buff with the other side of the cloth, avoiding a high shine. Let dry for seven days before walking on your finished floorquilt. It will take around a week for the finish to completely cure.

A Word about Water-Based Finishes

Water-based finishes have significantly improved over the years, and with advancing technology, newer additions of user-friendly water-based finishes are constantly appearing on the market. These finishes often consist of acrylic, polyurethane, or a mixture of both. The addition of polyurethane to the acrylic in some mixtures makes the finishes more durable and more flexible—ideal for a floorquilt. The finishes have become tough competition for the hardy long-trusted oil-based finishes. Unlike the oil-based finishes, however, the water-based finishes will not yellow with age. As well, any odors (if any) are at a minimum, and the drying time is considerably less. Never mix an oil-based finish with a water-based, and only apply a water-based finish over your (water-based) decoupage medium. Always allow the finish to completely dry between coats. Depending on the humidity, this could take anywhere from 6 to 24 hours. I always allow the *polycrylic* finish to dry for 24 hours between applications.

This beautiful fabric, "Fiesta Flower" by Maria Kalinowski (Canvas/Benartex), is protected with several coats of a decoupage medium and a water-based polyurethane. The floorquilt can quickly and easily be wiped clean should a spill occur.

Floorquilt Care & Handling

Floorquilts are easy to care for, and can quickly be wiped clean with a rag and water (and mild soap if needed) should a spill occur. As with any floor covering, it is best to wipe spills as soon as they occur. Floorquilts are spill-proof, but not entirely waterproof, so never place your floorquilt outside.

If you will be placing furniture (not too heavy) on your floorquilt, use feet protectors or large felt pads to protect the finish. The acidic water from house plants can also damage the finish, so avoid placing potted plants on your floorquilt.

If your floorquilt is placed in high traffic areas, you will want to remove the paste wax around every six months. Use a mild household cleaner, and reapply the wax as instructed on page 28.

Always place your floorquilt over a thin smooth non-skid rug pad, or apply a non-skid backing, such as *Saf-T-Bak* (sources on page 93). This will prevent your floorquilt from slipping and sliding. You can also use a *removable mounting putty,* found in the stationary departments of stores. Place pea-sized dabs under the edges (two inches in), then step on your floorquilt's edges to press the putty onto the floor.

To renew the appearance of your floorquilt, you may want to re-poly once every two years or so. Simply give your floorquilt a good cleaning, removing all wax with a mild household cleaner. Let it dry completely before applying one or two coats of water-based finish as directed on pages 27 and 28.

To prevent damage to the finish, always keep your floorquilt flat, or if it is large, *very* loosely rolled (with the design facing outward) when transporting or storing.

"Summer Bloom"

A Basic Beginner's Project made up of Circles & Squares

(Finished Floorquilt Size: 24" x 36")

With traditional quilting, a beginner would be advised to avoid a design that has curves, however, with floorquilting, circles are not a problem. The circles, squares, and contrasting colors that make up this simple geometric pattern produce a well-balanced design that will inspire you to feel confident enough to explore new designs to your own preference and satisfaction. There is no end to what you will be able to think up and create. Designs are as varied as the people who create them. So expand on your creativity with this basic design, and don't forget to have fun as you do!

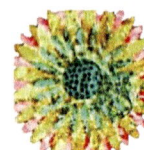

"I started floorquilting, and now my floors are in pieces."

Materials

■ Necessary tools & materials (see page 7)

■ Prepared 24" x 36" canvas (see pages 17 and 18)

■ Prepared fabrics—one yard of darker colors (for border, squares, and circles), and ½ yard of lighter colors (for squares and circles), a combination of colors and prints that you enjoy, and that will harmonize with the room your floorquilt will occupy (see page 12)

■ Three transparent plastic template shapes—one 6" square, one 5½" circle, and one 2" or 3" circle (see page 11)

Template Shapes

A gridded cutting mat can help you trace accurate template squares. You can use a math compass for the circles. Place the compass at the center of some drawing paper, and pencil 2¾" from the center a full 5½" circle. Trace the circle onto a plastic template sheet, and cut. Use your compass in the same manner for the smaller circle. I traced around an old jar. See what you have in your home—a can, lid, bowl, or jar can all be used to trace circles.

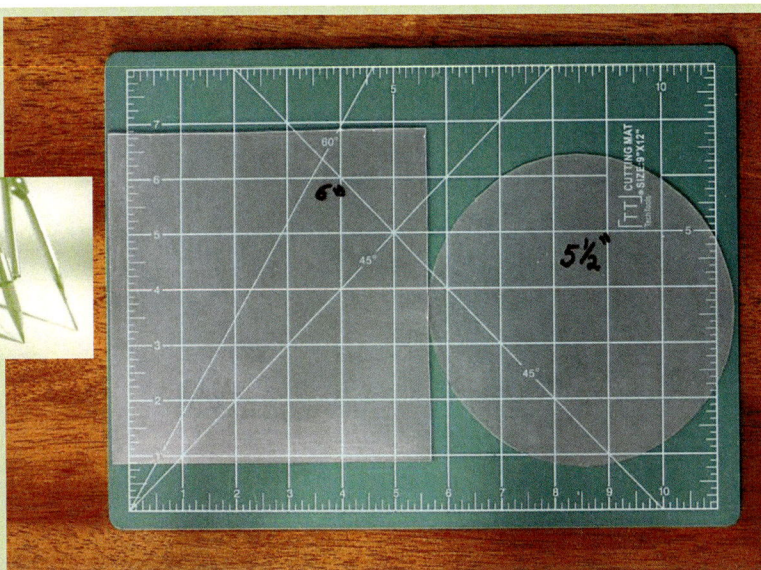

Note: *A circle cutter will cut circles from your fabrics more quickly and easily (see sources on page 93).*

How-To

1. Pencil a three-inch wide border on your prepared canvas, creating an 18" x 30" rectangle (see page 18, step 6).

2. From the border fabric, mark and cut (on the wrong side) four border strips: two strips 4" x 36" and two strips 4" x 26". Save enough fabric for eight 6" squares and seven 5½" circles.

3. Using the 6" square template and the 5½" circle template, mark and cut eight squares and seven circles from the wrong side of the border fabric.

4. With the 6" square template and the 5 ½" circle template, mark and cut seven squares and eight circles from the wrong side of the lighter fabric. Using the smaller circle template, mark and cut 12 small circles from the same lighter fabric. You can mark and cut several small circles if you desire. I cut (fussy cut) several small round flowers to accompany the smaller circles, which also consist of a single larger flower. You may engineer fabrics into leaves, butterflies, whatever you want.

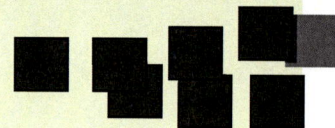

5. Following the photo on page 30, lay out all your square pieces within the 18" x 30" rectangle. *Check for proper placement, measurement, and alignment.*

After you have positioned all your pieces, you can keep track of each with a small piece of marked masking tape. For example, 1a could start the first block in the top row, 1b the second, 2a could start the second row, and so on. This is also helpful if you need to reassemble your pieces at a later time.

Press each square within the 18" x 30" rectangle, row-by-row (step 6).

6. Turn a corner square wrong-side up, and apply an *even generous* amount of *full-strength* decoupage medium onto the wrong side of the fabric. Turn the piece right-side up, and position it into place. Using a small lint-free rag (or your hand), press the square with short back-and-forth motions, taking care to smooth out *all* bubbles or wrinkles, no matter how small. This is a crucial step in floorquilt construction. Do not rub the edges too hard for too long, or you might fray the fabric.

7. Repeat step 6 for the remaining 15 squares. Press each piece within the 18" x 30" rectangle–row-by-row (*alternate colors and align edges*). Following the pattern on page 30, apply the 5½" circles in the same manner onto the squares. The smaller circles can be placed wherever you desire.

8. Follow the instructions for applying borders on page 20.

9. Decoupage four circles—one onto each border corner, as shown on page 30. You can add additional circles or smaller squares along your border if you desire—whatever you want.

10. Follow the instructions for applying the protective coatings and backing on page 25. Let the coatings dry (and cure) for seven days before walking on your new handmade floorquilt.

Congratulations!

*The same techniques that were used to create "Summer Bloom" were also used to create "Wild and Free." The floorquilt was easily constructed with 4" and 6" squares, and 2" and 5½" circles, featuring a lovely horse print (Way out West 2 "Wheat") from Robert Kaufman fabrics. Before you construct your next floorquilt (**one is never enough**), why not look at the traditional quilting patterns on pages 85–89, where you will find simple attractive designs, utilizing the most basic geometric shapes.*

"Bear's Paw"

A Traditional Pattern made up of Squares & Triangles

(Finished Floorquilt Size: 27" x 34")

After squares, triangles are probably the most frequently used shape in patchwork. "Bear's Paw" or "Bear's Track" has always been a popular pattern, composed entirely of squares and triangles. Inspired by the pattern's name, the shapes have been made more interesting by the use of warm earthy colors, bear, track, and berry prints. The traditional sawtooth inner border unifies and enriches the over-all design. A section of a larger version of "Bear's Paw" with sashing strips can be found on page 38. See also page 39 for a contemporary variation to this well-loved design.

"Where else would you find a bear's paw 'print' but on the floor."

Materials

- Necessary tools & materials (see page 7)

- Prepared 27" x 34" canvas (see pages 17 and 18)

- Prepared Fabrics—one yard of small darker prints (for border and 12 seven-inch squares), and three to four fat quarters (18" x 22") or ¼ yards of different fabrics—a balancing combination of colors and prints (one conversational, such as bears or tracks) that complement the border fabric (see page 12)

- Four transparent plastic template squares—one 7" x 7", one 2" x 2", one 1" x 1", and one ¾" x ¾" (see page 11, and box on page 31)

How-To

1. Pencil a three-inch wide border on your prepared canvas, creating a 21" x 28" rectangle (see page 18, step 6).

2. From the border fabric, mark and cut (on the wrong side) four border strips: two strips 4" x 34" and two strips 4" x 29". Save enough fabric for 12 (7" x 7") squares.

3. Using the 7" x 7" square template, mark and cut 12 squares—7" x 7" from the wrong side of the border fabric.

4. With the 2" x 2" template, mark and cut 48 (2" x 2") squares—12 from one fabric (conversational or novelty) 12 from the second complementary fabric, and 24 from the third fabric (small prints, such as leaves, etc.).

5. From any of the fabrics (except the border fabric), trace and cut 19 (2" x 2") squares for the inner border. Keep these separate from the other squares. I place mine in a clear zipper freezer bag marked *Sawtooth Border.* Match colors to distinguish the inner border.

6. To construct the one-inch squares, place a 1" x 36" yardstick on the wrong side of your desired fabric. Trace both sides of the ruler until you have a total of 96 (1" x 1") squares—48 from one fabric and 48 from another. That will be one 1" x 36" and one 1" x 12" strip from each fabric. Cut out your strips. Place your 1" square template at the start of each strip, and cut out each 1" square, as you move your template along the strip. Trim any uneven sides while your template is against the cut square.

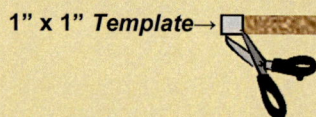

1" x 1" *Template*→

7. After the squares are trimmed, cut each in half diagonally—from one corner to the other. The squares are so small that one snip of the scissors is all it takes to make a clean even cut.

8. Cut 12 separate ¾" squares for the center of each 7" square. I will refer to these as *central squares.*

9. Time to decoupage! Using your sponge brush, apply full-strength decoupage medium to the wrong side of a 7" x 7" square. With an old rag, press the square, and each 7" *decoupaged* square thereafter, within the 21" x 28" canvas rectangle—row-by-row, taking care to smooth out *all* bubbles or wrinkles. *Align all edges and corners.* Do not rub the edges too hard for too long, or you might fray the fabric.

Start from the center and work your way outward (see step 10).

10. Lay out all the pieces that make up a one block pattern onto a "middle" square, as shown in the photos. Check for placement and alignment, then decoupage the ¾" *central square* onto the center of the block. This square will act as a guide for all the other pieces in the block.

Note: You can find the center of each 7" square by making a small pencil hole in the center of a 7" x 7" piece of graph paper. Place the paper upon each fabric square, and mark the very center.

11. Following the photo, decoupage four 2" squares from your conversational and complementary fabrics, making sure that each corner meets with the *central square* corners.

12. Decoupage four 1" half-square triangles along the outer edges of the 2" squares, as shown in the photo. Match colors to distinguish each completed *Bear's Paw*.

13. Continue steps 10–12 for each of the 12 blocks. **Work your way from the middle squares outward, watching for placement, alignment, and accuracy**.

14. Follow the instructions for applying borders on page 20. See step 15 below for inner border.

15. Using a ruler, cut each of the 19 squares for the inner sawtooth border diagonally—from one corner to the other—creating four triangles from each square. Decoupage the triangles onto the inner edges of the outer border, as shown in the photo on page 34. Start at the center of each side, and line up the triangles. Check for placement "before" you decoupage. **Corners**—apply two triangles to each corner, as shown on page 34.

16. Follow the instructions for applying the protective coatings and backing on page 25.

Wait around seven days (allowing the finish to cure) before stepping on your bear's paw prints.

Sashing square

Sashing strips

Each block in this quarter section of a 29" x 65" "Bear's Paw" floorquilt is separated by red sashing strips. The continuous and short strips create a latticework effect, which unifies the over-all design. Further interest has also been added with the use of small brown sashing squares, placed at the inner corners of each block (see box on page 24).

Variation on a Theme (Floorquilt Size: 25" x 37")

There is no end to the designs that you can create with traditional patterns. This "Bear's Paw" floorquilt was easily planned on graph paper. Each square on the paper represents one inch on the floorquilt. See what you can create, or follow the pattern below. Work your way from the center outward—starting with the centered 11" x 11" bear fabric ("Bears Paw" by Robert Giordano, Giordano Studios). If you would like to construct your own bear for the center, please see the template patterns on pages 40 and 41. The border is made up of two 2" x 37" strips and two 2" x 27" strips. Work your way outwards, and apply the border "before" you add the "outer" bear paws.

Optional Pattern for *Bear's Paw* Variation, page 39
(For 11" x 11" Center Block)

Butterfly (Trace wings face down and up for a total of four wings.)

Flower stem, center, & petal

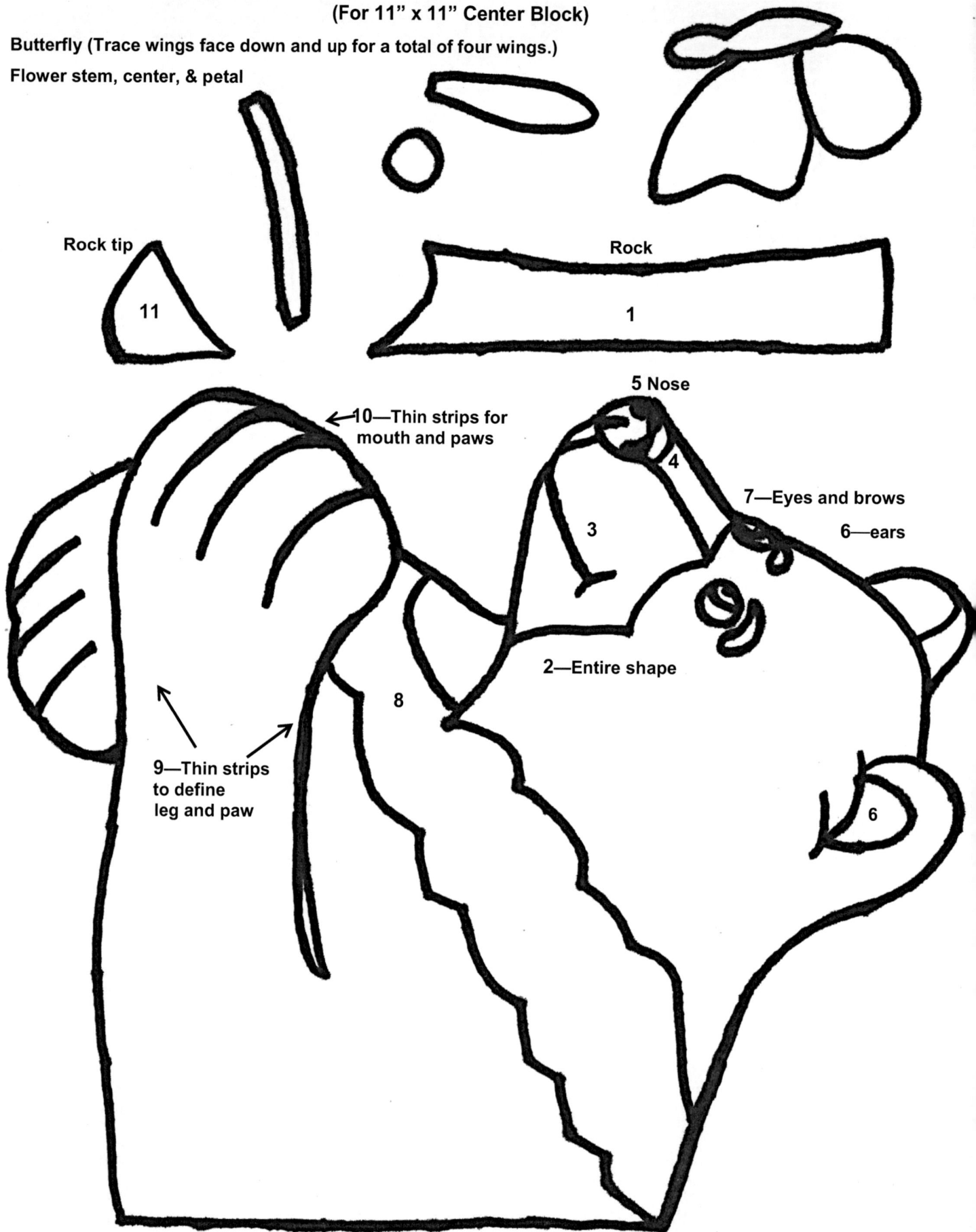

Rock tip

11

Rock

1

5 Nose

4

3

7—Eyes and brows

6—ears

10—Thin strips for mouth and paws

2—Entire shape

8

9—Thin strips to define leg and paw

6

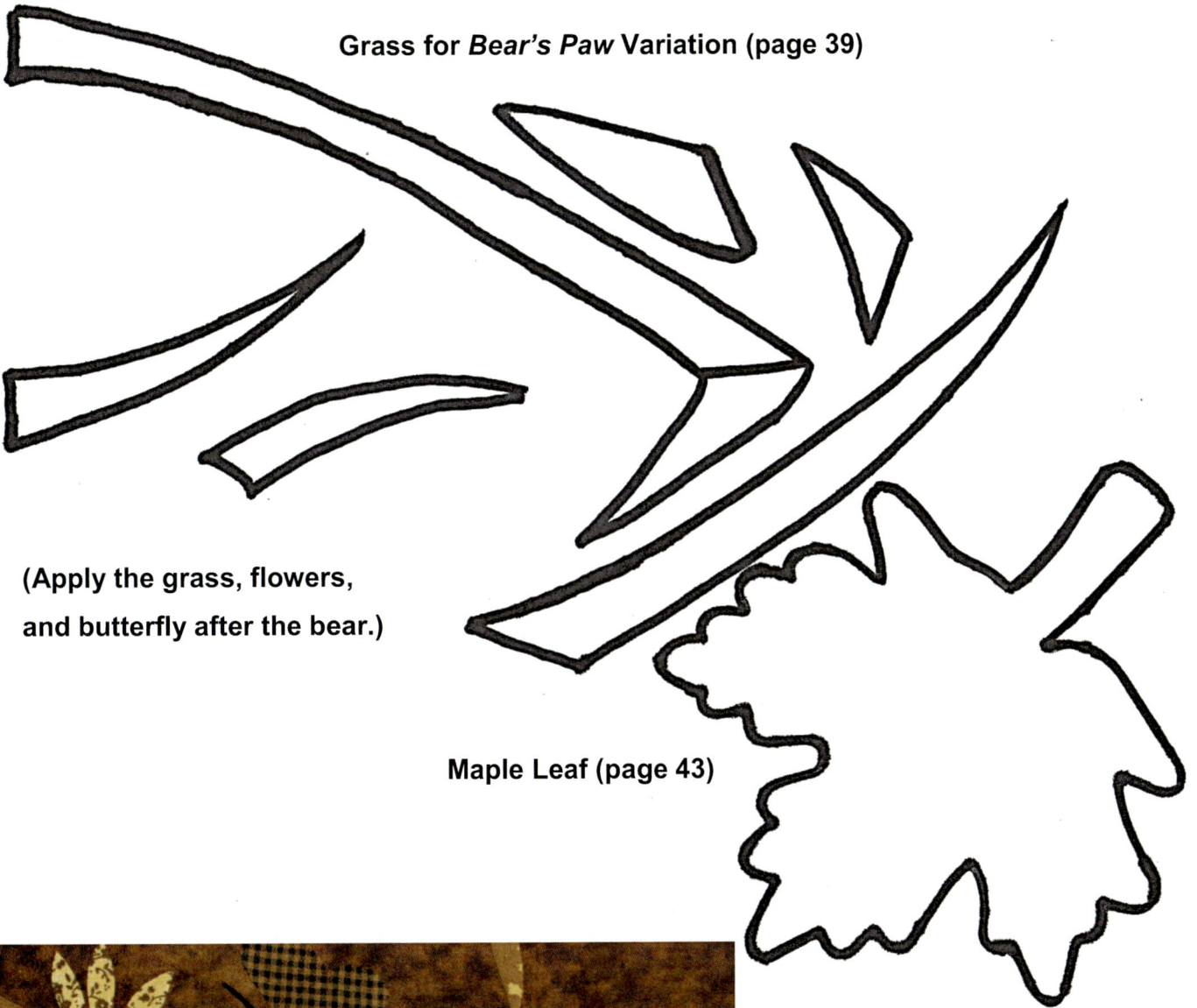

(Apply the grass, flowers,
and butterfly after the bear.)

Maple Leaf (page 43)

*11" x 11" center block—
an optional pattern for
a "Bear's Paw" floorquilt*

Use a clear plastic template
sheet to trace the patterns. When
marking your treated fabrics,
place your template shapes face-
down on the wrong side of the
fabrics. Cut and decoupage the
treated fabric pieces for the bear
in the order in which they are
numbered.

It's Nice to Know!
The Friendship Quilt

Many early American women gave quilts as personal and practical gifts. Each friend and/or family member would design and personalize her own block. To help harmonize the over-all design, a basic motiff was usually chosen, such as a wreath with green foilage. When pieced together, the blocks resulted in a beautiful and memorable quilt. These quilts were highly treasured, and used only on occasion, and as a result, many examples exist today. Why not get together with your family and friends, and make a "friendship floorquilt." Use a basic color scheme and design concept (see What's in a Block? on page 9). Then have each person (especially children) design and appliqué a basic motif, such as a flower or a teddybear, in any color or print of their choosing. What a fun way to get together with family and friends!

"Friends are like fabric—you can never have enough!"

Idea!...

Make a colorful play mat! Children love when we turn colorful cotton fabric panels into durable fabric decoupaged play mats—no wrinkles and the toy cars sail across the fabric. There are many fabric panels available— from alphabet and roadway themes to construction and princess themes. Why not see what playful fabric panels your favorite fabric store carries.

More Fun with Squares & Triangles

"Maple Leaf Creek"   (Floorquilt Size: 24" x 36")

These traditional and contemporary maple leaves look as if they are floating in a shadowy mountain creek.

To make: First pencil a one-inch wide border on your treated canvas. Second, decoupage (in order) your background fabric (22" X 34", page 45—step 5) and border (two 2" x 26" and two 2" x 36" strips, page 20). The leaves are made up of two-inch and one-inch squares, and two-inch and one-inch half-square triangles. The two-inch squares of the smaller leaves are cut at the corners, using a one-inch square template. Cut the one-inch squares in half—diagonally for the edges. The pattern for the contemporary maple leaf is found on page 41. Follow the directions on page 25 when applying the protective coatings.

"Crazy Patch Apples & Sashing"

(Finished Floorquilt Size: 24" x 36")

Crazy patch quilts are patchwork quilts that consist of small odd-shaped pieces of fabric. The fabric is carefully pieced together in a seemingly random or crazy manner of sizes and colors. In this contemporary version of a crazy patch quilt, the crazy patch apples are framed by sashing strips that run continuously along the full diagonal length of the quilt (see box on page 24). To help unify the design while adding further interest, small apple leaves have been applied to the background fabric and borders.

"When life throws you scraps—make a crazy patch floorquilt!"

Materials

■ Necessary tools & materials (see page 7)

■ Prepared 24" x 36" canvas (see pages 17 and 18)

■ Prepared fabrics—1½ yards of a darker small print (for border, sashing strips, and eight small apple pieces), ½ yard of a lighter small print (for background), and four fat quarters or ⅛ yards of darker complementing colors and prints (for apples and leaves), see page 12

■ Transparent plastic template apple and leaf shapes (see page 11, and patterns on page 76)

How-To

1. Pencil a three-inch wide border on your prepared canvas, creating an 18" x 30" rectangle (see page 18, step 6). *Accurate measurements are important here.*

2. From the border fabric, mark and cut (on the wrong side) four border strips: two strips 4" x 36" and two strips 4" x 26".

3. From the same border fabric, mark and cut (on the wrong side) 8 sashing strips—two strips 1" x 12¾", two strips 1" x 11¾", and four strips 1" x 25".

4. *Accurately* mark and cut from the wrong side of the lighter background fabric an 18" x 30" rectangle.

5. Apply a *generous* even amount of full-strength decoupage medium onto the 18" x 30" canvas rectangle. Carefully press the 18" x 30" piece of light fabric (right side up) within the rectangle. Using your rag, *thoroughly* press with back-and-forth motions, smoothing your way from the fabric's center to the corners and edges. Spread the medium onto any fabric edges outside the penciled rectangle. Let dry.

6. Pencil a light mark (on the canvas) nine inches from every corner along the 18" x 30" rectangle. Mark also three inches from the corners on each of the longer sides of the fabric rectangle. The sashing strips will start and end at these marks.

7. Position the corner of each decoupaged 1" x 12¾" strip on the 9" marks at the center of each shorter side of the 18" x 30" fabric rectangle. Place the opposite corners of the strips on the 9" marks along the longer sides of the fabric rectangle, as shown in the illustration below.

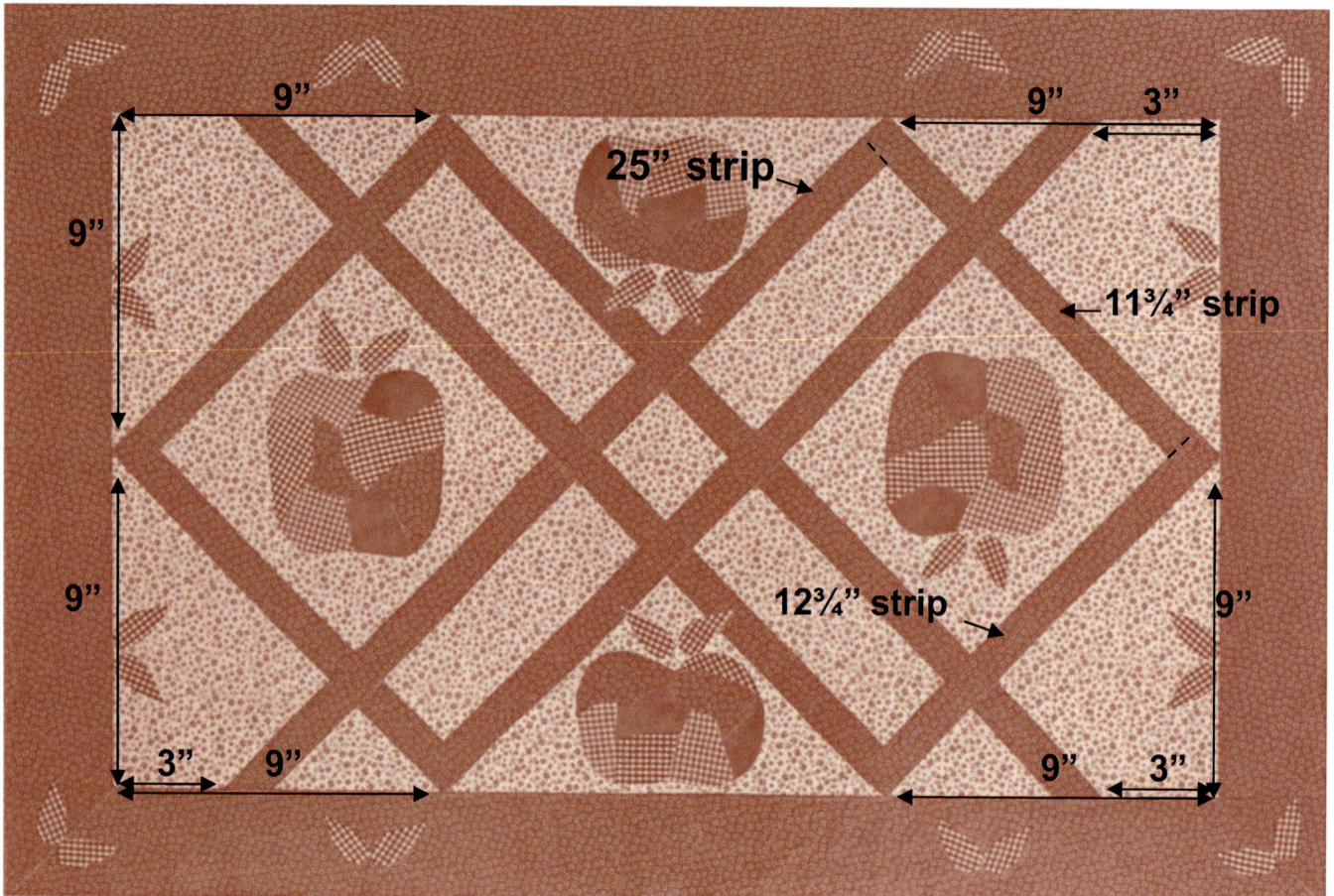

8. Position the short edge of each decoupaged 11¾" strip against the inner long edge of the 12¾" strips (as shown at the right), while placing their opposite corners on the 9" marks along the long sides of the fabric rectangle, as shown above.

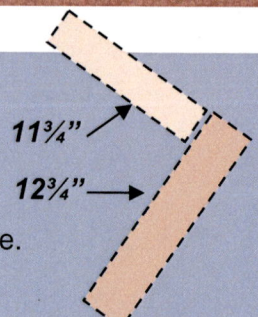

9. Decoupage the four long 25" strips against the inner corner edges of the shorter 11¾" and 12¾" strips, positioning the opposite ends at the three-inch marks on the longer sides of the fabric rectangle, as shown in the above illustration. Trim the ends at the three-inch marks even with the edges of the fabric rectangle.

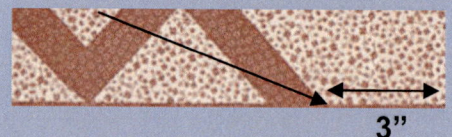

10. Follow the instructions for applying borders on page 20.

Note: To cut the corners so that they appear mitered, see the top of page 47.

The corners can be cut to appear mitered, where the two strips overlap. Just place your ruler diagonally from the corner edge, and cut the top strip overlap by a 45% angle, as shown in the photo at the right. Then proceed with the instructions for applying borders on page 20.

11. After constructing the two apple templates, mark and cut each into eight sections, as shown in the photo below. You can make these crazy patch puzzle-like pieces any shape or size you like.

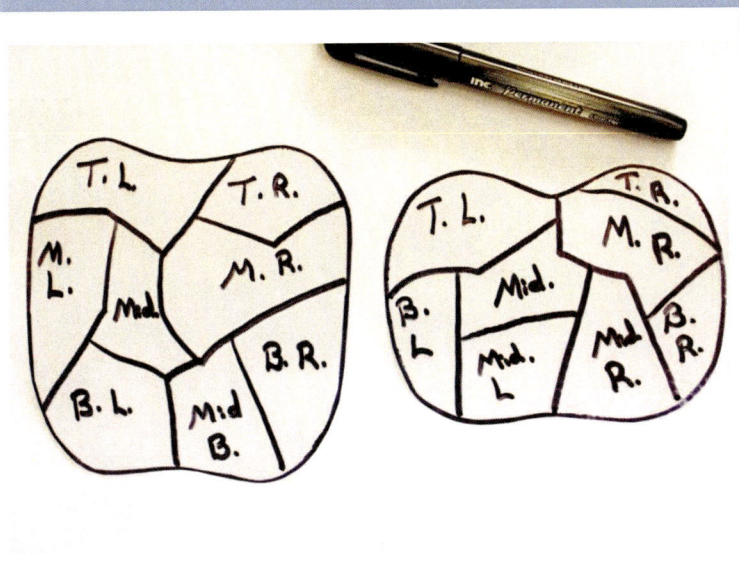

Mark each crazy patch piece, as shown in the left photo—T.L. for top left, B.R. for bottom right, and so on. This will make it much easier to re-piece the shapes at a later time. You can keep track of your fabric pieces in the same manner with small bits of marked masking tape.

12. Mark and cut, on the wrong side of four different fabrics (for apples), two shapes from each fabric per apple. This will be a total of 32 pieces—eight for each apple. You can, of course, make as many apples as you want!—apples, flowers, butterflies, hearts—whatever you wish to create.

13. Following the photo on page 44, decoupage the apple pieces onto the background fabric, between the sashing strips, or wherever you prefer.

14. Use the leaf pattern (page 76) to make your template. Mark (on the wrong side of your fabric), cut, and decoupage 32 (or more if you like) apple leaves, as shown in the photo on page 44.

15. Follow the instructions for applying the protective coatings and backing on page 25.

"Grandmother's Flower Garden"

Hexagonal patchwork

(Finished Floorquilt Size 24" x 36")

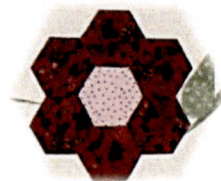

Hexagons are used to create many geometric designs, which can easily be planned on graph paper that is ruled in hexagons. As a sewed quilt, "Grandmother's Flower Garden," with its dozens of colorful hexagons, would require lots of skill, time, and intricate piecing. As a floorquilt, however, this old-time favorite can successfully be mastered, petal-by-petal, in a fraction of the time. My version of "Grandmother's Flower Garden" can easily be adapted to the design, colors, and prints of your own choosing. See also page 89 for hexagonal butterfly patterns.

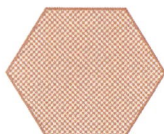

"A grandmother's flower garden has love in every petal."

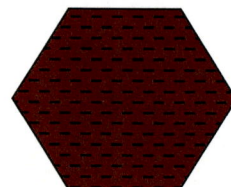

Materials

- Necessary tools & materials (see page 7)

- Prepared 24" x 36" canvas (see pages 17 and 18)

- Prepared fabrics—½ yard of a darker solid or small print (for border and hexagons),
½ yard of a light color (for background and hexagons), and three to four ¼ yards of colorful fabrics (for hexagons, leaves, and stems) that complement the border and background fabrics (see page 12)

- Hexagon and leaf template (template patterns on page 76, see page 11)

- One transparent plastic template sheet for stems (see page 11)

- Graph paper ruled in hexagons (see sources on page 93 for free download)

How-To

1. Plan your design on graph paper ruled in hexagons (see page 93 for free download of paper). I started my design in the very center of the paper, and worked outward, marking with letters and colored pencils each hexagon—P for pink, R for red, W for white, and so on (see drawing). **Each hexagon on your graph paper will be the equivalent of around 1½" on your canvas.**

Note: Pre-cut hexagonal templates can be found in the quilting sections at fabric and craft stores (page 11). The hexagon template pattern is located on page 76. *Hexagonal butterflies* are on page 89.

2. Pencil a three-inch wide border on your prepared canvas, creating an 18" x 30" rectangle (see page 18, step 6).

3. From the darker border fabric, mark and cut (on the wrong side) four border strips: two strips 4" x 36" and two strips 4" x 26". Save enough fabric for 68 one-inch hexagons. These are gray in the photo on page 48.

4. Using the hexagonal template, mark and cut 68 one-inch hexagons from the wrong side of the border fabric. **Be as accurate as possible when marking and cutting—making sure the sides are even, and the corners are sharp**. For a more precise cut, hold the template against the fabric while cutting.

5. From the white (or light) fabric, mark and cut an 18" x 30" rectangle from the wrong side of the fabric. Save enough fabric for 74 one-inch hexagons.

6. With the hexagonal template, mark and cut 74 hexagons from the wrong side of the white (light) fabric, 101 hexagons from the wrong side of the colorful (red) fabric, and 60 hexagons from the wrong side of the other colorful (pink) fabric.

7. From the green (complementary) fabric, mark and cut several leaves (using the leaf template) from the wrong side of the fabric. The stems will be cut to your desired size after the hexagons are decoupaged, using the plastic template sheet.

8. Time to decoupage! Spread a *generous* even amount of full-strength decoupage medium onto the 18" x 30" canvas rectangle. Carefully press the 18" x 30" piece of light fabric (right side up) within the rectangle. Press the fabric with a small rag, using short back-and-forth motions until the entire piece is "well-adhered" to the canvas. Spread the medium onto any fabric edges outside the penciled rectangle.

9. Follow the instructions for applying the borders on page 20.

10. Using a ruler, find the center of your canvas from each of the border's inner edges, and decoupage your first colorful (red) hexagon exactly on the center point (9" from the top/bottom, and 15" from the sides), following the drawing on page 51. **Make sure the corners of your hexagon are pointing the same direction as in the photo on page 48, and make *double* sure of your measurements.**

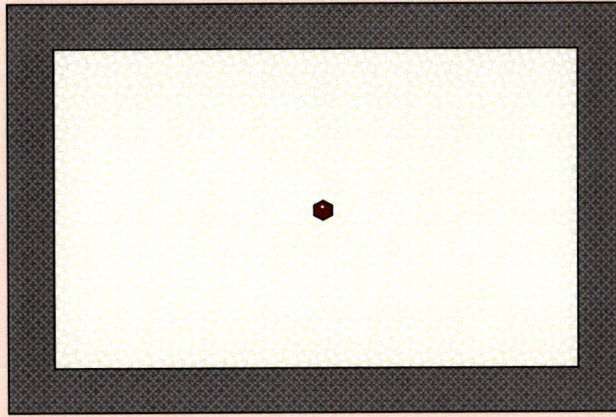

11. Working from the center hexagon outward, decoupage the remaining hexagons, as shown in the photo, or according to your own design. **Use your ruler, take your time, and make sure each hexagon is even on all sides.** If a piece needs to be larger or smaller, use your template to mark and cut another piece to the required size. Keep in mind—fabric can stretch. If a hexagon is just *slightly* uneven, work the piece with your fingertips into the desired position. The edges may also slightly overlap if necessary.

12. With the plastic template sheet, mark and cut several stems. If you want your stems to travel from flower-to-flower, place the template sheet over the flowers to mark the correct distance. Do not make the templates too narrow. If you want the exact stem on both sides, use only one template per size. When you have finished tracing the stem onto the wrong side of your fabric, simply turn the template over, and trace it again. You will now have two stems that are the same size and shape for both sides of your design (see page 11). Using the stem templates, trace (on the wrong side of your fabric) and cut your fabric shapes.

13. Decoupage your stems and leaves according to the illustration, and/or to your own design and liking. Construct and apply as many as you desire.

14. Follow the instructions for applying the protective coatings and backing on page 25.

Remember to wait around seven days after the protective coatings have dried

before walking in your Grandmother's Flower Garden!

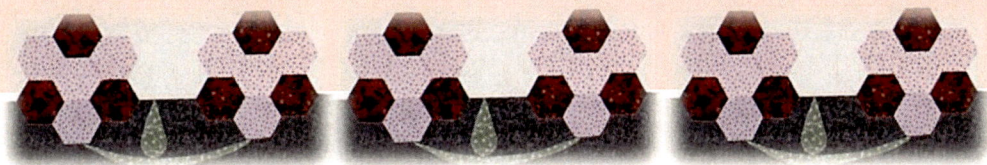

"Floral Dreams"

Cat & Kitten Whimsical Patchwork with Curved Strips

(Finished Floorquilt Size 24" x 36")

Here is fun example of how patchwork and appliqué can be whatever you want—another way to play with shapes, colors, and prints. This whimsical patchwork cat and kitten, with their colorful combination of floral strips, small prints, and gentle curves, can easily be personalized to the design and color scheme of your choosing. So go ahead! have fun! with your fabrics. Your creativity will be spinning around and around!

"A family is a patchwork of love."

Materials

- Necessary tools & materials, including a math compass (see page 7, and box on page 31)

- Prepared 24" x 36" canvas (see pages 17 and 18)

- Prepared fabrics—½ yard of a smaller darker print (for border), ½ yard of a complementary larger and lighter print (for background), several fat quarters or ¼ yards of small darker prints (for cats), and pink and black scrap pieces for noses, tongues, and eyes (see page 12)

- One large poster board, and two large sheets of transparent template plastic (see pages 11, and 77-79)

How-To

1. Pencil a three-inch wide border on your prepared canvas, creating an 18" x 30" rectangle (see page 18, step 6).

2. From the border fabric, mark and cut (on the wrong side) four border strips: two strips 4" x 36" and two strips 4" x 26". Save the remaining fabric for strips on both the cat and kitten.

3. On the poster board (using the compass), mark a large circle—17" in diameter (or less or more)—for the cat. Place the compass at the center of the poster board, and pencil 8 ½" from the center a full circle, as shown in the drawing below. I just happened to have a round laundry basket that was the correct size, and used it to make my template. See what you have around your home. A large bowl or lid, for example, could likewise be used to create a circular template. Mark the size of your templates for future use.

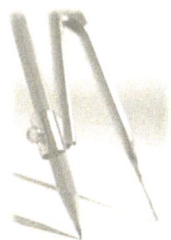

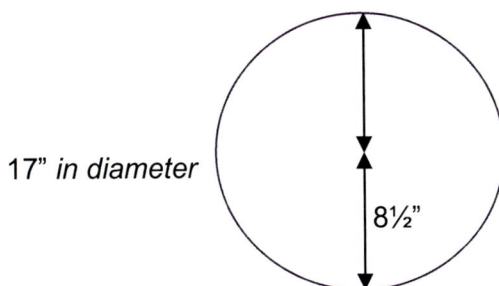

17" in diameter

8½"

An inspiring design similar to *Floral Dreams (utilizing fabric strips)* can be found on page 56.

4. Starting towards the bottom-right of your circular poster board template (*using your compass*), pencil 4–5 curved horizontal lines for the cat's thigh (around 1"–2" apart). Then starting from the left of the circle (above the horizontal lines), mark 10–11 slightly curved vertical lines (narrow to wide, 1"–2" apart) for the rest of the cat's body. The first section at the left (the chest) will be wider. Mark each of the sections—1t-to-5t for thigh sections, and 1b, 2b, and so on for body sections. Cut out these labeled templates.

Draw the first section of the thigh towards the bottom right of the circle, as shown in illustration #1. After the thigh strips have been drawn, draw the vertical strips, starting from the left, as shown in illustration #2. Cut out these templates.

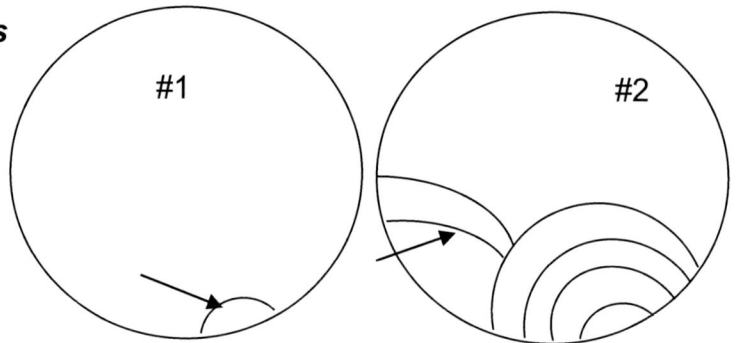

5. Using the two plastic transparent template sheets and patterns on pages 77 and 78, trace and cut the cat's face, facial features, feet, and tail (read caption on page 55). You can enlarge the face and/or facial features with a scanner, computer, and printer if you desire. Do the same for the kitten (pages 78 & 79). Remember to mark your template shapes *right side,* and any hard to distinguish features (see page 11). Save smaller pieces in clear plastic zip lock bags for safekeeping.

6. From the background fabric, mark and cut (on the wrong side) an 18" x 30" rectangle. Mark and cut four small 3" circles also for the corners of the border.

7. Apply an even and *generous* amount of decoupage medium onto the 18" x 30" canvas rectangle. Carefully press the 18" x 30" piece of light fabric (right side up) within the rectangle. Use your rag, and *thoroughly* press with short back-and-forth motions, smoothing your way from the fabric's center to the corners and edges. Spread the medium onto any fabric edges outside the penciled rectangle. Let dry.

8. Follow the instructions for applying your borders on page 20.

9. Using the poster board templates, placed right side down on the wrong sides of the fabrics (for the cat's body), carefully trace, cut, and label each piece. You will use two templates for each piece of fabric.

10. With the face, facial features, tail, feet, and kitten plastic templates (placed right-side down on the wrong sides of your chosen fabrics), trace, cut, and label each piece of fabric. Trace the cat's and kitten's eyes, ears, face stripes, and whisker templates right-side up and down to insure symmetry (read caption below).

Patterns for the plastic templates are found on pages 77–79. One template for each different facial feature is all that is needed. After you trace the template right-side up, turn the template over, and trace again. You will now have the same symmetrical shape, such as a facial stripe, for each side of the face.

11. Time to decoupage the cat! Lay out all your marked pieces for the cat's body. Following the photo on page 52 and drawings on page 54, decoupage the pieces onto the background fabric, starting with the bottom horizontal thigh piece. After the thigh pieces, decoupage the vertical body pieces, starting with the wider chest piece at the left. Decoupage the head next, positioning it nearly half-way over the top of the chest, as shown in the photo. To prevent darker fabrics from showing through lighter fabrics, follow the information at the bottom of page 15. I personally like the fabrics showing through.

12. Decoupage the kitten and feet. Position the pieces so that the kitten's head touches the cat's chin.

13. Decoupage the facial features (both cats), starting with the round cheeks, as shown in the photo.

14. After you decoupage the four corner circles, follow the instructions for applying the protective coatings on page 25. Wait around seven days before walking on your new whimsical floorquilt!

"Greatest Gifts," one of my first floorquilts, was inspired by my old and loyal friend—Mopsy Baby. To keep the fabric smooth and flat, the cat's circular (17") body was decoupaged directly onto the canvas before the strips of colorful scrap remnants were cut and applied.

Scrap Happy Stripes

Stripes can add a warm cozy effect when used on the floor. Mimicking a hand-made braided rug in a rustic country setting, a floorquilt constructed with multi-colored fabric strips is very inviting and pleasing. Creating such a quilt is also an excellent way to use up scrap remnants of fabrics. The key to creating a fabulous striped floorquilt is to cut your strips straight and accurate. If you are working on a gridded mat, use the lines on the mat to make a straight cut. If you use a rotary cutter, align your ruler with the vertical grid line and tracings. Cut along the ruler and away from yourself. If you prefer curved strips, see the techniques used in *Curiosity* (page 57).

"Curiosity"

Garden Pond Pictorial Appliqué

(Finished Floorquilt Size 24" x 36")

A pictorial quilt can permanently capture cherished scenes and memories for all to enjoy. Whether a realistic interpretation or artistic, these quilts are often simplified, using the most basic and prominent shapes. To recreate your favorite scene or picture, just make a copy of the photograph (which will act as a guide), and outline the major shapes. Enlarge the shapes, such as rocks, plants, and animals to the desired size. The artistic shapes in "Curiosity" were kept simple, and are easily recognized as grass, water, fish, lilies, and of course—a curious cat.

"When one walks with nature, one receives far more than he seeks."—John Muir

Materials

■ Necessary tools & materials (see page 7)

■ Prepared 24" x 36" canvas (see pages 17 and 18)

■ Prepared fabrics—½ yard of bright vivid colors (for border), four ¼ yards of complementary colors for water, and several ¼ yards or fat quarters for the grass, koi, water lilies, and cat—a balancing combination of colors and small prints that complement the border and water fabrics (see page 12)

■ Two large poster boards (around 22" x 28"), and two large transparent plastic template sheets (Template patterns are on pages 80 and 81.)

How-To

1. Pencil a 3-inch (long sides) by 2-inch (short sides) border, creating an 18" x 32" rectangle on your prepared canvas.

2. Lightly pencil a vertical line six inches in from one side of your rectangle. This 6" x 18" section will be the grass. The larger 18" x 26" rectangular section will be the pond.

3. From the border fabric, mark and cut (on the wrong side) four border strips: two strips 4" x 36" and two strips 3" x 26".

4. If not already the correct size, mark and cut from your poster board an 18" x 26" rectangle. Referring to the photo on page 57, draw nine curved lines (vertically) inside the poster board rectangle, creating ten waves.

For the water, draw nine wavy lines within the 18" x 26" poster board (see photo on page 57).

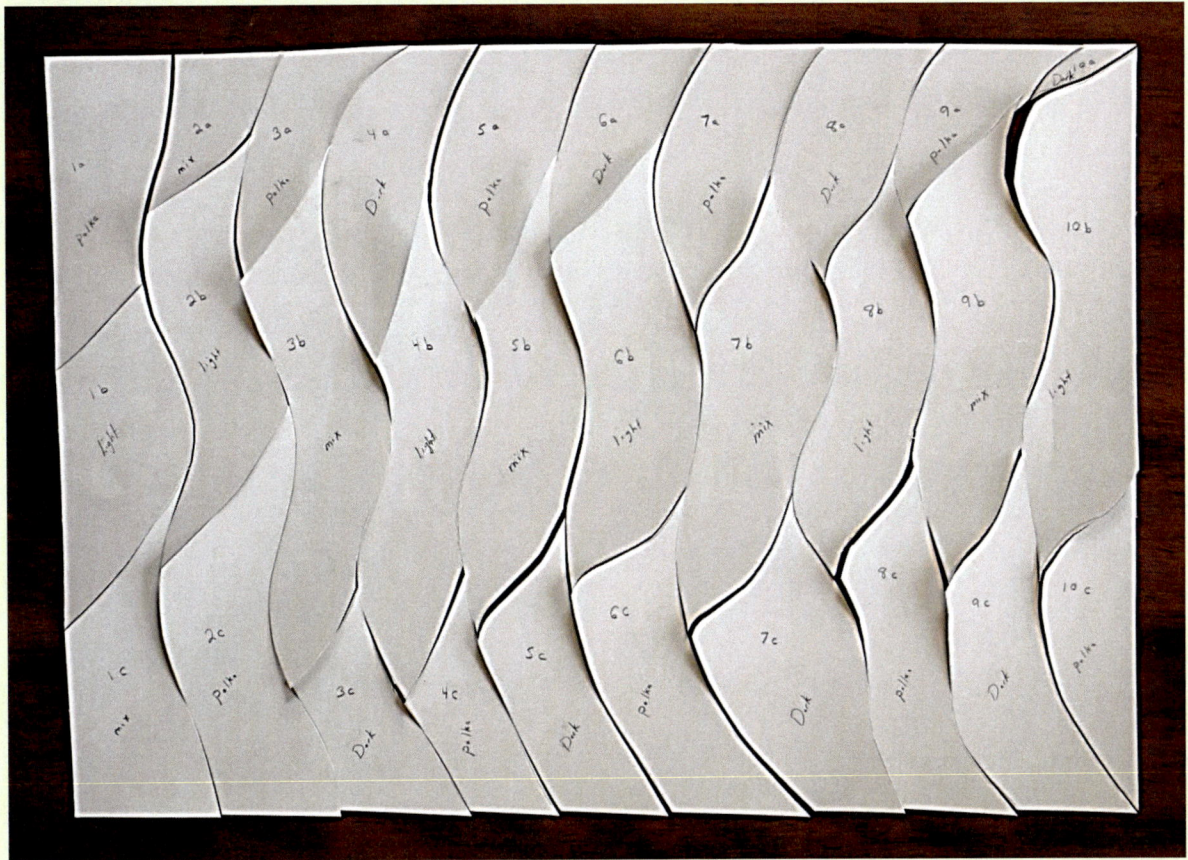

5. Within each curved wave, draw three slightly curved lines (creating three sections), as shown in the photo. Label each of the three sections within the ten waves. The first wave will be labeled 1a, 1b, and 1c. The second will be 2a, 2b, and 2c. You will also want to mark the chosen fabrics (for the water) onto each section to avoid any confusion. Keep lighter colors in the middle sections.

6. Carefully cut out the poster board sections, keeping all your numbers in order.

7. Place each poster board section right-side down onto the wrong side of your chosen fabric for the pond's water, and accurately trace the shapes. Label the wrong side of each piece of fabric with masking tape the same as its poster board template.

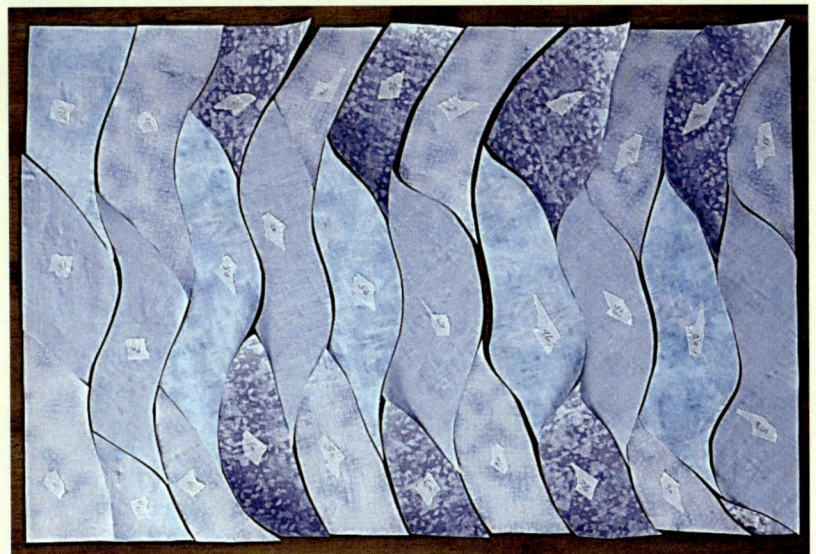

8. Carefully cut out each fabric shape, keeping all your numbers in order.

9. To construct the grass and flower lawn, mark and cut from another poster board a smaller 6" x 18" rectangle. Draw six curved lines within the rectangle, similar to how you created the waves for the pond. Label and cut out these template shapes. Follow steps 7–8, using two alternating fabrics for the lawn. Use the border fabric for the one shape that extends from the border to the lawn.

10. For the lily pads, trace the template patterns on page 81 onto your transparent plastic template sheet. Cut and mark each of the lily pad's five sections—1–5. Using two different fabrics, place each template right-side down onto the fabric's wrong side before tracing. To create the water lilies, trace ten petals for each flower, repeating a bright color found in the border fabric (pattern for petal on page 81).

11. The template patterns for the cat, fish, and water rings are found on pages 80 and 81. These can be enlarged if you choose, using a scanner, computer, and printer. Only one template is needed for the cat's symmetrical features, such as the eyes. Trace the shapes onto a transparent plastic template sheet, and then cut out your pieces. Remember to turn your templates right-side down when tracing on the wrong side of the fabric. When tracing the cat's eyes onto the fabric, trace one with the template upright, and the second eye with the same template turned over. Do the same with each different sized stripe to ensure symmetry. Trace the small rings of water that encircle the koi onto the lightest of the pond water fabrics. Use fabric colors that will help distinguish the cat and koi, while yet balancing your color scheme.

12. Time to decoupage!

Lay out all your pieces for the pond water in order. Starting with the first wave section, decoupage each piece within the larger 18" x 26" rectangle. You will begin with piece 1a in one corner, and end with piece 10c in the opposite corner.

13. Decoupage the grass pieces (1–6) inside the smaller 6" x 18" rectangle, as shown in the photo. Let the medium dry thoroughly before the next steps.

14. Follow the instructions for applying borders on page 20.

15. After your borders have dried, decoupage the cat onto the edge of the grass lawn and border, as shown in the photo. If the fabric is a lighter color, you may want to cut out another (cat) shape, and decoupage it onto the wrong side of the cat fabric to prevent any darker fabrics from showing through (see bottom of page 15). I personally like the colors showing through. Apply the facial pieces next, starting with the bottom of the face, and working your way to the stripes on the tail. You can add as many stripes as you like. Pay close attention to the eyes, which will ultimately portray the curious cat.

16. Decoupage the koi, as shown in the photo. Use the tip of your finger to apply the mouth and eyes. Press each positioned piece with a dry rag to secure into place. Apply the water rings, as shown.   (Water Rings)

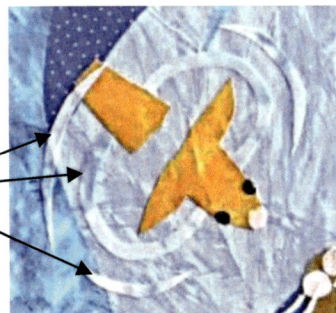

17. Decoupage your lily pads and water lilies, as shown in the photo. You can also fussy-cut flowers or leaves from the border fabric, and place them slightly over the water's edge, adding even more realistic and colorful elements. Remember, you are the artist. Why not add a dragonfly? or a boulder? The possibilities are endless, so go ahead and expand your creativity to your own preference and desire.

18. To finish your floorquilt, follow the instructions on page 25 for applying the protective coatings.

Remember to wait around seven days before dipping your toes on your new garden pond!

Using Stained Glass Patterns

Stained glass patterns have been used by quilters for many years. Rather than mimic true stained glasswork, I enjoy using the patterns to create a more realistic effect. The huge variety of decorative patterns can range from a single curled leaf, to an elaborate forested landscape. When searching for patterns, choose those that are simple, and that use a minimum number of shapes. Patterns are available in books, magazines, and on the web. Many online glasswork stores carry "free" stained glass patterns. When searching for stores, simply type "stained glass patterns" on your search engine. I made the colorful koi above, using a simple pattern from "Glass Crafters" (Pattern by Laura Heathcote, "Glowing Panes Glassworks" and "Spectrum Glass"). The pattern, which also suggests colors, consists of only a few easy-to-cut shapes.

(**Note:** Always get permission before selling or giving away items constructed from patterns that are not from you. Let the owner know what you intend to use the pattern for. They often do not mind, as long as you get permission.)

It's important to understand that nothing can replace your own creative designs, which are true expressions of you, resulting in original one-of-a-kind works. Don't worry about how well you can draw. Your personal style will reveal much charm and character. I must admit that although I enjoy using stained glass patterns, I have more fun creating my own patterns, such as the fish I designed in "Curiosity" with its wide open mouth, portraying *Whiskers*–my favorite kissing koi (page 57). My final advice: *"Have fun, dare to be creative, and never expect perfection."*

Constructing the Templates

After you have acquired your stained glass pattern, you will want to construct templates. Before you begin, read *A Word about Templates* on page 11. Place the clear template sheet on top of the pattern, and using a black permanent marker, outline the shapes that you want to use in the pattern. The pattern to the iris below included a background that I was not interested in, so I only outlined the flower, which consists of ten simple easy-to-cut shapes. Carefully cut out each shape. Then place each plastic template shape where it belongs on the paper pattern. Number each template (on the upright side), so that you can remember the order in which they are placed. Position your templates right-side down on the wrong side of your treated fabrics before tracing. Accuracy is crucial here. If a shape does not properly fit, use your fingertips to gently work the decoupaged fabric shape into place. It's also alright to overlap the fabrics. This produces an extraordinary look. So once again, I stress, *have fun with your fabrics!*

.................Idea!

Have any coloring books lying around? The simple child-like outlines found in these can also be used as unique patterns. You can make templates from the outlines just as you would with stained glass patterns. So the next time you walk by some coloring books at your local store, why not take a second look!

Iris pattern by "Spectrum Glass"

Make a Sampler Floorquilt (Floorquilt Size 26" x 37")

Quilters often enjoy making sampler quilts. A sampler quilt is made up of many different patterns. The beautiful patterns that make up this cheery "sampler floorquilt" were designed after very popular historical block patterns. The blocks are named (from left): Flower Basket (Flower Pot), Rainbow, Pine Tree (variation), Pinwheel & Butterfly, Colonial Cottage (Little House), Rose Garland (variation), Log Cabin, Grandmother's Flower Garden, Four-in-Nine Patch, Maple Leaf, and Sunbonnet Sue. To create such a floorquilt, you will first need to pencil a design similar to the one on page 65. Full scale patterns to Rose Garland, Rainbow, Butterfly, and Sunbonnet Sue are found on pages 82 and 83. The hexagon for Grandmother's Flower Garden is found on page 76. You may want to substitute the blocks for your own favorite patterns (see page 85). Just remember that one square on your graph paper is the equivalent to one inch on your floorquilt. Don't forget to check out the hundreds of historical patterns that have been preserved throughout the years for us to remember, construct, and enjoy for many more years to come....

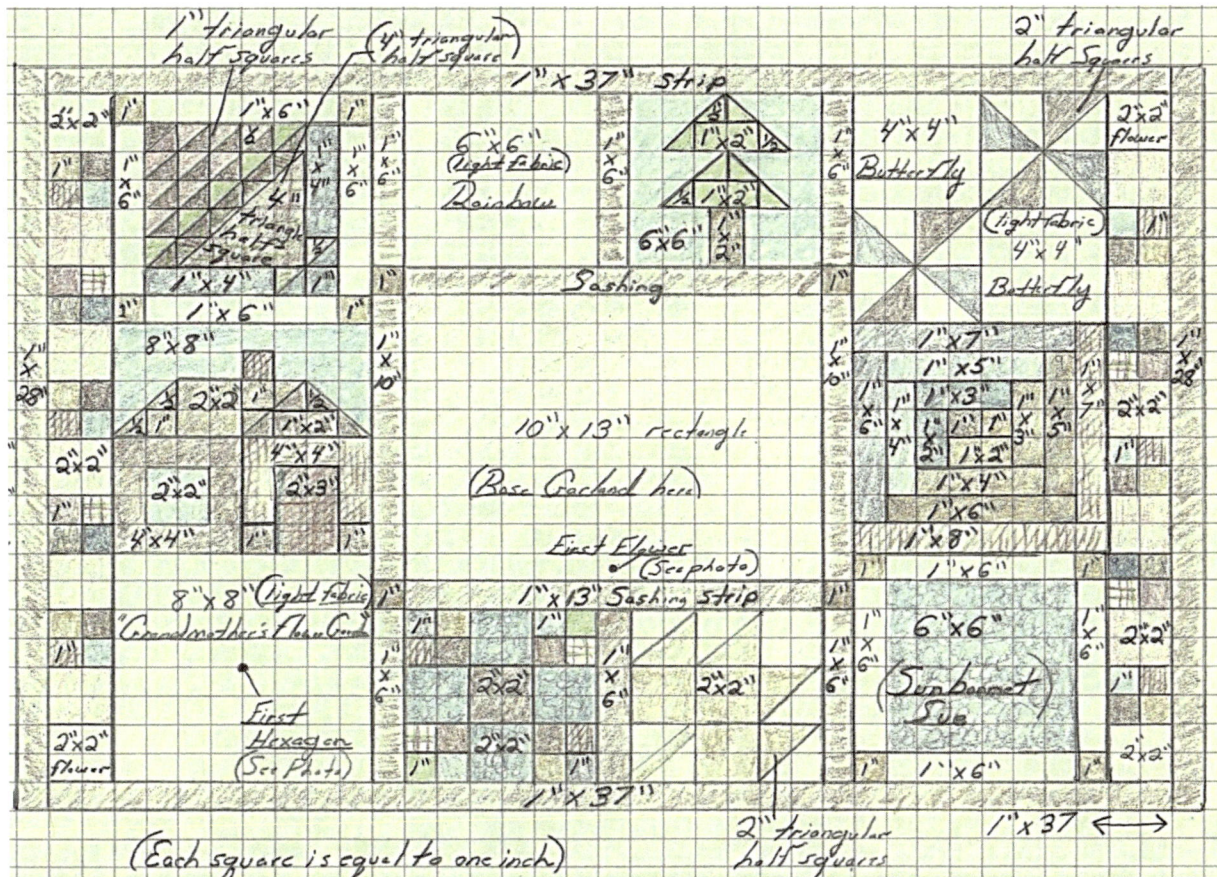

1" triangular half squares (4" triangular half square) 2" triangular half squares

2"x2" 1" 1"x6" 1" 1"x37" Strip 2"x2" flower

1" x 6" 6"x6" (light fabric) 1" x 6" 1"x2" 4"x4" Butterfly

Rainbow

4" triangular half square 6"x6" 1"x2" (light fabric) 4"x4"

1"x4" 1" 1" Sashing Butterfly

1"x6"

8"x8" 1"x10" 1"x7"

1"x5"

2"x2" 1"x2" 1"x3"

2"x2" 4"x4" 10"x13" rectangle 1"x2" 2"x2"

2"x2" 2"x3" (Rose Garland here) 1"x4"

4"x4" 1"x6"

First Flower 1"x8"

(See photo) 1"x6"

8"x8" (light fabric) 1"x13" Sashing Strip 6"x6"

"Grandmother's Flower Garden" (Sunbonnet

Sue)

2"x2" 2"x2" 2"x2"

First 2"x2" 1"x6" 2"x2"

2"x2" Hexagon

flower (See Photo) 1"x37"

(Each square is equal to one inch) 2" triangular half squares 1"x37"

Materials

- Basic tools and materials (page 7), two clear template sheets and patterns on pages 76, 82, and 83

- Treated 26" x 37" canvas (pages 17 and 18)

- Treated Fabrics (page 12): two 2" x 28" strips and two 2" x 37" strips (darker color with small prints for border), two 1" x 13" strips, two 1" x 10" strips, and six 1" x 6" sashing strips (from the border fabric), one 10" x 13" rectangle (a lighter color for central block), and fabrics for squares, triangles, hexagons, rectangles, and template shapes—a balance of colors that complement the border and sashing (see above design for sizes and shapes)

How-To

1. After you create and color your design on graph paper, lightly pencil the outline (border and squares) on your treated canvas, as shown above (one inch = one square). Next, make templates from the patterns (see pages 76, 82, and 83).

2. Mark and cut out all the shapes from your chosen fabrics. Trace the butterfly wings and rose garland templates face down and up on the fabric's wrong side to ensure symmetry of each piece (see page 11, and photo on page 64).

3. Decoupage the central 10" x 13" fabric rectangle first, then decoupage the rose garland and surrounding blocks, as shown. ***Pay close attention to accurate measurements.*** Lastly, add the sashing strips and borders. (See page 20 for border application, and page 25 for applying protective coatings.)

Have a Furry Family Member?

Floorquilts can be used in a variety of settings, including those for our four-footed friends. As attractive pet dish mats, these functional floor coverings can be quite effective in protecting our floors from messy eaters. If you would like to personalize a dish mat that you plan to make for your furry family member, use the alphabet template pattern on page 84 for names, quotes, whatever you prefer! Decoupage the letters onto your floorquilt as you would with other fabric pieces. The simple following project (on page 67) will inspire you to get started. Remember to clean your pet dish mat whenever spills occur.

All for Our Four-Footed
FRIENDS

"Paw Prints & Patches" Pet Dish Mat (16" x 24")

Materials

- Basic tools and materials (page 7), including template letters of your choosing (pages 11 and 84)
- Treated 16" x 24" canvas (page 17)
- Treated Fabrics: one 10" x 18" rectangle (novelty print), two 4" x 18" and two 4" x 24" strips (small print), and one fat quarter or ¼ yard of a vibrant solid print for letters and paw prints (see page 12)

(To construct the paw print templates, simply draw on a small template sheet, one large circle and one small circle, similar in shape to those above or to your preference. These can be used to construct the 4 paws and 16 toes.)

How-To

1. Pencil a three-inch wide border on one side of your treated canvas, creating a 10" x 18" rectangle.

2. Brush an even *generous* coat of full-strength decoupage medium onto the penciled rectangle. Next, press and smooth the 10" x 18" treated fabric rectangle within the penciled rectangle until *well-adhered.*

3. Follow the instructions on pages 21–23 for applying the borders.

4. Using the templates, trace and cut out your desired letters (and paw prints, as shown). Trace the letters face down on the fabric's wrong side (page 11). Apply the shapes, using full-strength decoupage medium and an old rag. Lastly, follow the instructions on page 25 for applying the protective coatings.

"Off-the-Floor" Projects

From reversible bookmarks, coasters, and placemats, to seasonal table runners and scenic wall hangings, the same attractive fabrics and designs that beautify our floors can also be used to create a variety of durable and practical "off-the-floor" items. Such projects are an excellent way to use up scrap remnants of fabric. Smaller projects, such as bookmarks, can be constructed with just two layers of treated fabric, decoupaged back-to-back, then coated and sealed as you would a floorquilt. Larger projects are made with canvas in the same manner as a floorquilt, only you do not need to apply a non-skid additive or backing. So go ahead! grab your scrap bag of fabrics, browse through the inspiring ideas and projects ahead, and see what you can create to your own imagination and liking.

This reversible bookmark was made with just two layers of treated scrap fabric decoupaged back-to-back over strips of decorative yarn. The narrow border and horse were applied before the fabric was coated and sealed with a decoupage medium and a water-based finish (as you would a floorquilt).

Chinese Lattice Scenic Wall Hanging (Pattern on page 70)

Floorquilts can also be hung as durable wall quilts. Three sets of medium-size damage-free hanging strips will secure a 24" x 36" floorquilt to just about any wall. I decided only to frame the beautiful scenic background fabric above, which consists of one solid piece of fabric, decoupaged directly onto a treated canvas. The Chinese lattice design is made up of several lengths of one-inch wide strips, which creates a unique three dimensional effect.

Eventually, you may come across a spectacular fabric that you could never get yourself to cut. Not all fabrics were meant to cut up. If that happens to you, simply allow the design to determine the size your floorquilt. Frame your fabric with a border or a lattice design that supports the beauty of the fabric without causing distraction. Graph your design before you begin. Why not use the following Chinese lattice design pattern on page 70.

"Keep a green tree in your heart, and perhaps a singing bird will come." —Chinese Proverb

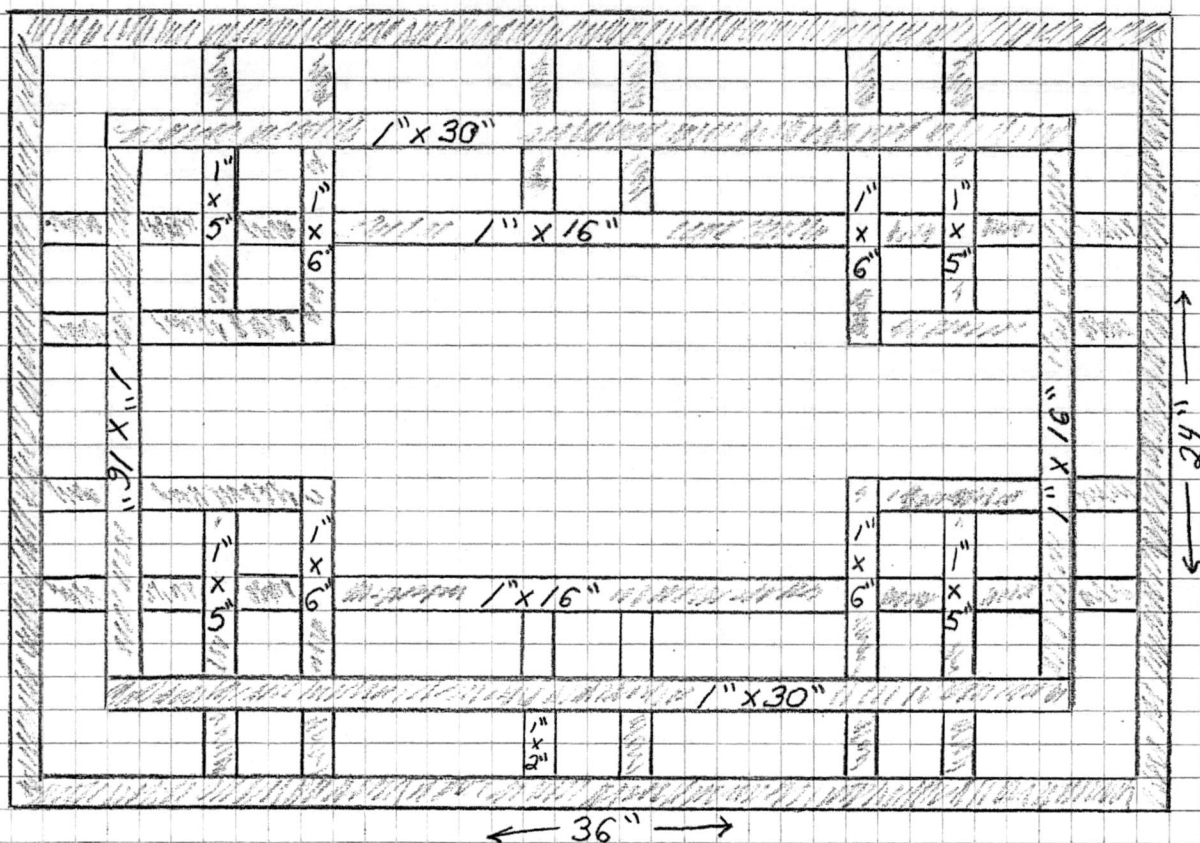

Chinese Lattice Design 24" x 36" (Page 69)

This fun maze-like design can easily be constructed with the following treated fabric strips (see page 12)—two 2" x 26" strips and two 2" x 36" strips for border, two 1" x 30" strips, four 1" x 16" strips, four 1" x 6" strips, eight 1" x 5" strips, and thirty-two 1" x 2" strips.

Cut your strips *straight* and *accurate*.

To ensure proper placement and alignment, always use a ruler. Apply your two-inch border strips first, over your central design (see pages 19 and 69). Instructions for applying borders are found on pages 20–23. When your borders are adhered, measure five inches in from each inner border edge and corner. This is where you will decoupage (full-strength) your first 1" x 2" strips. Measure another two inches over for the next 1" x 2" strips. After you decoupage the two-inch strips along the inner sides of your borders, apply two 1" x 30" and 1" x 16" strips against the 1" x 2" strips. Continue working from the outside inward, placing the strips as shown in the drawing. *Carefully measure* as you move along. If you should come across a strip that does not fit properly, simply measure and cut a new strip to the correct length. When you are finished, follow the instructions for applying the protective coatings on page 25. Remember, you do not need to apply a non-skid additive or backing for a wall hanging. Damage-free hanging strips can be found at most hardware and department stores.

Bookmarks & Bag Tags

Materials

- Basic tools and materials (page 7)

- Leftover treated fabrics (see page 12):

Bookmarks—two 2" x 5" strips, two 1" x 5" strips, and two 1" x 2¼" strips (*longer bookmark and narrow border—two 1½" x 6" strips, two ½" x 6" strips, and two ½" x 2¼" strips*), and a small shape, cut from treated fabric, such as a butterfly or flower

- A few strips of decorative yarn or ribbon (optional)

Bag Tags—two 3" x 3" squares, two 1" x 3" strips, and two 1" x 3¼" strips (include several inches of ribbon)

How-To

1. Apply full-strength decoupage medium to the wrong side of two 2" x 5" strips (for bookmark) or two 3" x 3" squares (for bag tag).

2. Lay the ribbon or yarn (optional for bookmark) on the decoupage medium—½" to 1" from the upper edge of one 2" x 5" strip. Adhere the second strip (or square for bag tag) onto the first (over any ribbon), back-to-back, pressing each side with your fingers to ensure proper adhesion.

3. Fold all four border strips in half, length-wise (wrong sides facing inward). Apply decoupage medium to the inside of the folded 1" x 5" strips (1" x 3" for bag tag). Press the folded strips over and onto the right and left edges of your bookmark or bag tag—creating a ½" border on both sides. Repeat this step with the last two strips, placing one each at the bottom and top. If you are using yarn or ribbon, simply cut the top folded strip in half, then decoupage each half onto the top front and back of the bookmark. Snip off the excess folded overlaps before finger-pressing all sides of your border.

4. After you decoupage the small (fussy cut) shape to your liking (see photo above), follow the instructions on page 25 for applying protective coatings. If you are making bag tags, punch a hole in the corner with a hole puncher before applying the protective coatings. Lastly, tie a decorative ribbon, as shown in the photo to the right.

Want your initials? Use the alphabet pattern on page 84.

"Harvest Time!" Reversible Placemats (12" x 18")

Materials

- Basic tools and materials (page 7)

- Four 12" x 18" treated canvas rectangles (page 17)

- Treated Fabrics (page 12): eight 11" x 17" rectangles from a lighter color, eight 2" x 14" and 2" x 18" border strips, eight 1" x 14" and 1" x 6" inner border strips from a darker color, and colorful treated scraps from leftover projects for the stems, leaves, cupcakes—whatever you like!

How-To

1. Pencil a one-inch border on each side of your canvas rectangles. Apply an even *generous* amount of full-strength decoupage medium within the penciled area on one side. Press an 11" x 17" fabric rectangle onto the canvas with an old rag until it is *well-adhered*. Repeat this step with the other canvas rectangles on both sides. After this, the backsides of each mat will only receive one-inch wide outer borders.

2. Fold your outer border strips in half, lengthwise (wrong sides inward). Next, follow the directions on pages 21–23 (steps 4–13). Decoupage your inner border strips one inch from within your outer border.

3. Cut the desired shapes from your treated scraps. See what you have. I had fun fussy-cutting *tasty cupcakes* from my treated scraps. Using full-strength decoupage medium, apply the shapes to your personal design and liking. Lastly, follow the instructions on page 25 for applying protective coatings.

Reversible Coasters

This lovely vibrant fabric by "Laurel Burch" was made up of nine different 3" x 3" squares—ideal for four 4½" to 5" reversible coasters. Each colorful square is supported and framed with treated leftover fabrics from previous projects. These durable coasters would make great personalized gifts for family and friends.

Materials

- Basic tools and materials (page 7)

- Four 5" x 5" treated canvas squares (page 17)

- Treated fabrics: eight 5" x 5" squares from a lighter color and non-distracting print, eight 1" x 5" and eight 1" x 5½" darker colored strips for borders, and eight 3" x 3" small decorative squares or other colorful shapes. Look at fabric panels online, and see what you can find. Sources are found on page 93.

How-To

1. Apply an even *generous* amount of full-strength decoupage medium to the wrong side of a 5" x 5" treated fabric square. Press the fabric square onto a canvas square with an old rag until well-adhered, then finger-press the edges. Repeat this step with the remaining squares.

2. Fold all 16 border strips in half, lengthwise (wrong sides facing inward). Next, apply full-strength decoupage medium to the inside of two 1" x 5" strips. Finger-press the strips over and onto the two opposite sides of a 5" x 5" square—forming a ½" border on both sides.

3. Apply full-strength decoupage medium to the inside of two 1" x 5½" folded strips. Finger-press the strips like before, creating a ½" border on each side, as shown in the photo. Snip off any excess folded overlaps, and finger-press each corner. Repeat steps two and three for the remaining 5" x 5" squares.

4. Decoupage the 3" x 3" decorative squares or other colorful fabric shapes onto the 5" x 5" squares, on both sides.

5. Follow the instructions for applying protective coatings on page 25. *To prevent your coasters from sliding, place them on small 4" x 4" squares, cut from rubber shelf liner.*

Problem Solving

Floorquilting is most often a trouble-free process, but occasionally problems do occur. Through trial-and-error, I have come up with the following solutions, though not infallible, to the most common problems that you may encounter while constructing your floorquilt.

Problem: Folds, creases, or ripples in the raw folded canvas

Solution: Press the canvas with a hot steam iron, set on cotton. Mist strong folds and creases before pressing. Do not worry about staining, as these will be covered with gesso primer. Sometimes strong folds do not disappear entirely. They will, however, lessen as the floorquilt is constructed. Depending on your design, slight ripples, creases, or wrinkles may be desirable, as they may better mimic the look of a true patchwork quilt. If possible, ask a retailer to "roll" your fabric, and not fold it.

Problem: Fabric not adhering properly to the canvas

Solution: Carefully lift or remove the piece of fabric from the canvas, and reapply a *generous* amount of full-strength decoupage medium to the wrong side of the piece. Press the fabric into position with an old rag, pressing with short back-and-forth motions. Do not rub too hard around the edges, or your fabric may fray. It is very important that you take the time to smooth out *all* air bubbles, no matter how small. Refer to page 20 (*Borders*) if you are having similar problems with your border.

Problem: Fabric will not align with another piece

Solution: Occasionally, no matter how careful and precise we are, the fabric pieces just do not properly fit. One side may be slightly uneven, or too short, etc. Sometimes the only thing to do is to retrace and cut another shape. Before you go through all that trouble, it is beneficial to remember that fabric is stretchable, especially moist decoupaged pieces. Use your fingers or a rag, and gently stretch the fabric into the desired position. It's also perfectly alright if the fabric edges just slightly overlap one another.

Problem: Uneven borders and unaligned patterns at corners

Solution: If the offending border strip (or strips) has not dried, you can simply lift it off, decoupage, and reposition it. If the border has already dried, apply an inner border, and corner squares (see page 24). These will help cover uneven edges on borders, and border patterns that just do not turn the corner as we would like. Small motifs can also be applied onto border corners and where block edges meet.

Problem: Air bubbles underneath the decoupaged fabric

Solution: This problem occurs for one or more of the following reasons: (1) the decoupaged fabric was not thoroughly pressed onto the canvas or another fabric. (2) The decoupage medium dried before adhesion took place. (3) The decoupage medium was not applied evenly, completely, or generously. (4) The decoupage medium did not *thoroughly* dry before the finish was applied. If you have not applied the water-based finish yet, use a needle to poke a hole in the bubble (releasing the air), then smooth the decoupage medium directly over the bubble. Finger-press the bubble, rubbing back-and-forth until the fabric sticks to the canvas. If the fabric has already been treated with the water-based finish, do nothing. Finish your floorquilt (and wax), allowing it to dry for 48 hours. Using a steam iron, set on cotton, place the problem area between two old **smooth lint-free** pillow cases (or similar *cotton/polyester* material) to protect the quilt, iron, and ironing surface. Warm the bubble with the iron—removing the iron every few seconds. The wax will slightly melt. Each time you remove the iron, quickly and carefully wipe and *press* (with circular motions) the warmed area and wax with the pillow case. The wax will be hot, so do not touch the area with your bare hand at this time. **Careful! Do not allow the iron to remain on the bubble beyond a few seconds at a time, or you will melt your finish, and possibly burn yourself. Keep young children away from any hot iron or material.** The air bubble should minimize as it is warmed and pressed.

Problem: Air bubbles, streaks, skips, or debris in the dried or drying finish

Solution: The following tips will help prevent tiny air bubbles from forming in the final coats of polycrylic (polyurethane and acrylic) or polyurethane finish: *(1) Never shake the finish container. (2) When you stir the finish, use a paint stirrer, and stir very slowly. (3) Keep your brush clean, and free of lint, tiny hairs, etc. (4) When applying the finish, make sure that the brush is well-loaded to avoid skips, which can also lead to bubbles (a wider brush helps). (5) Always apply an even coat steadily. (6) Do not brush for too long in one area. (6) Work in a bright clean area that is free of lint, pet hair, and other floating debris.* If air bubbles, streaks, or tiny debris are in the finish, allow the finish to completely dry, then lightly sand as you normally would. Sand the air bubbles and/or tiny debris until they are not as noticeable. *Do not sand into the dried decoupage medium, or you may damage your fabric.* Wipe away the dust, and apply your water-based finish as instructed. It is alright and even preferable to apply a fourth coat if necessary.

Patterns
for Templates

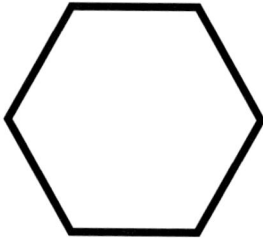

Hexagon, pages 48 and 64

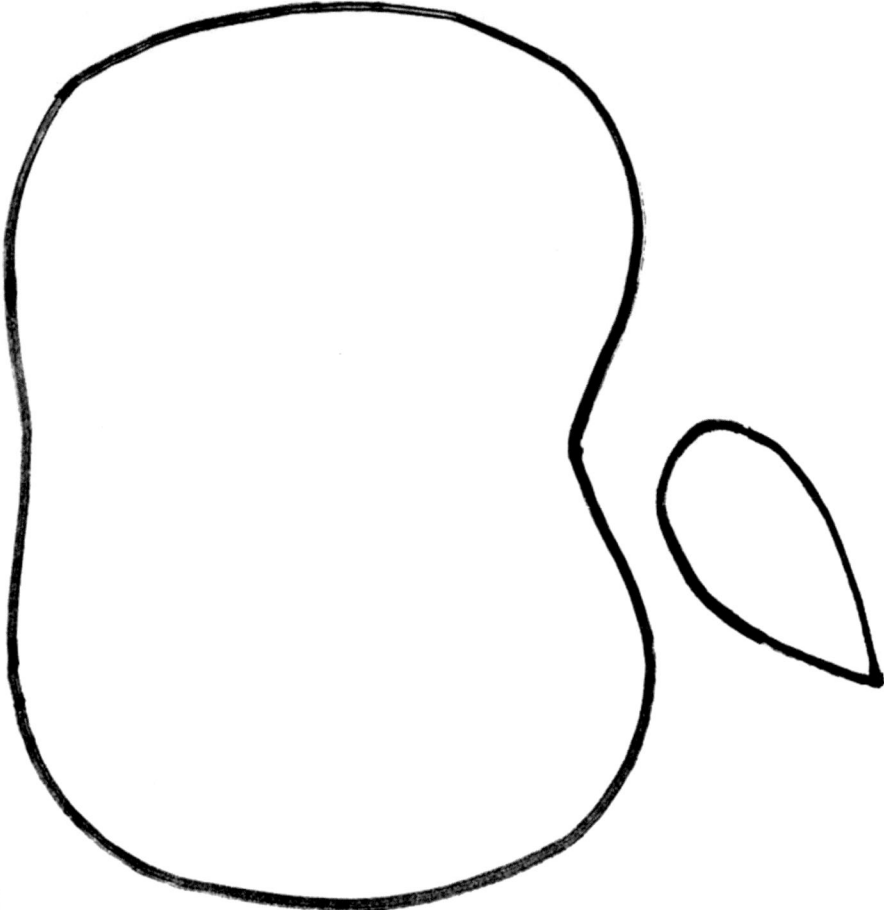

Crazy Patch Apples,
page 44

Floral Dreams Cat Head, page 52

Kitten Head

Cat Foot

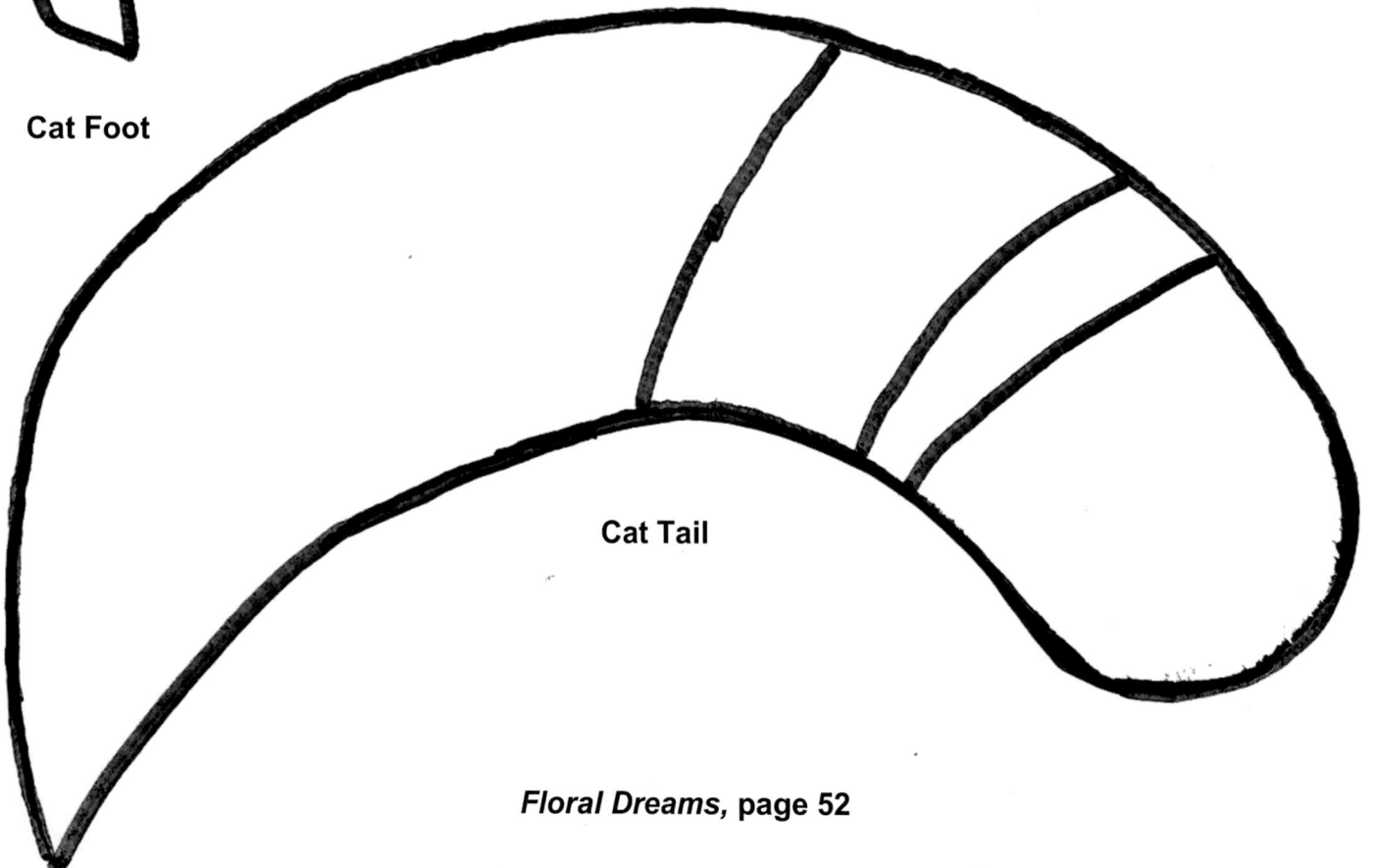

Cat Tail

Floral Dreams, **page 52**

Kitten Tail

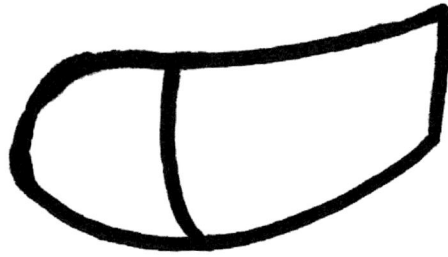

Kitten Foot

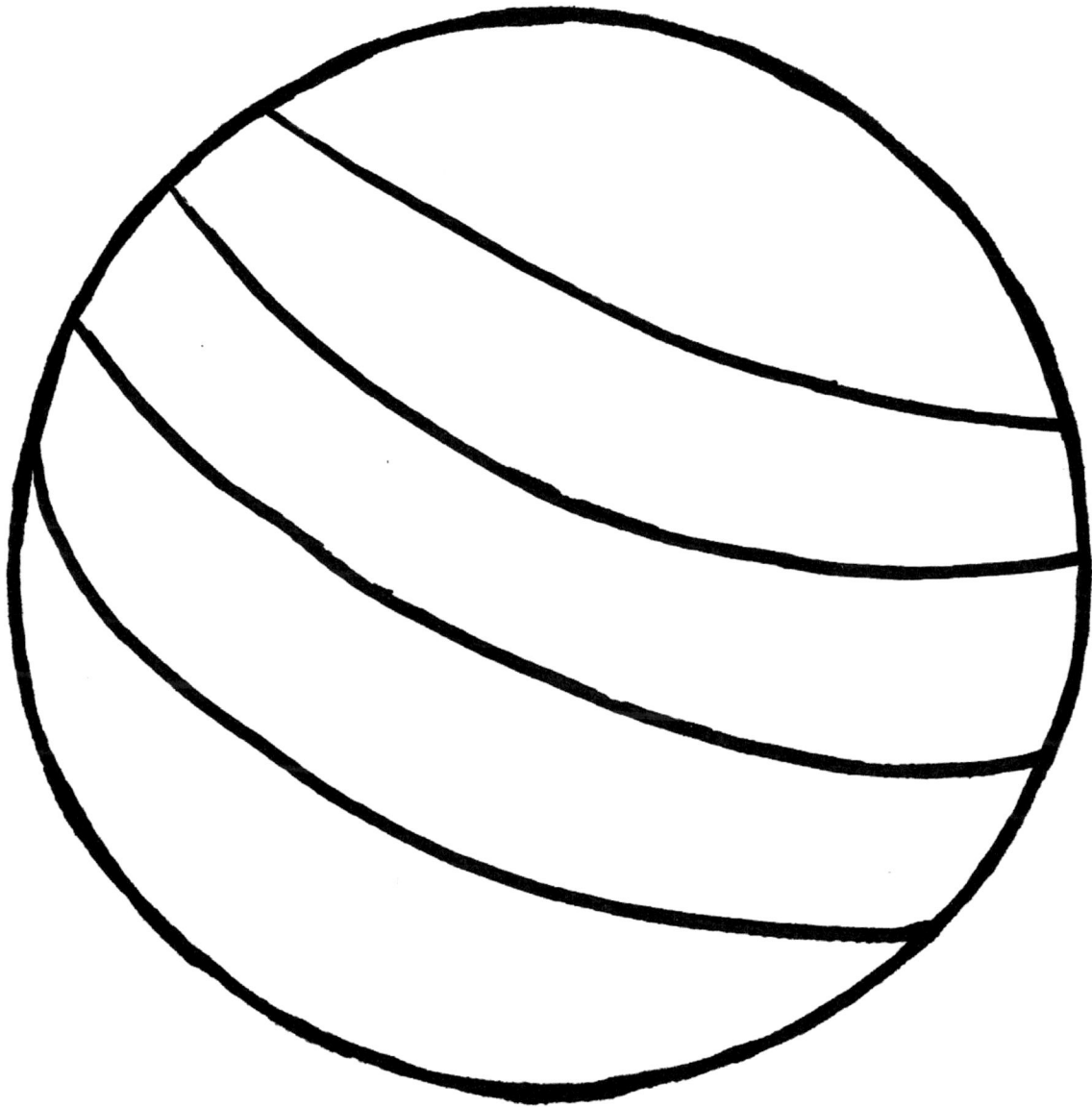

Floral Dreams **Kitten Body, page 52**

Curiosity Cat,
page 57

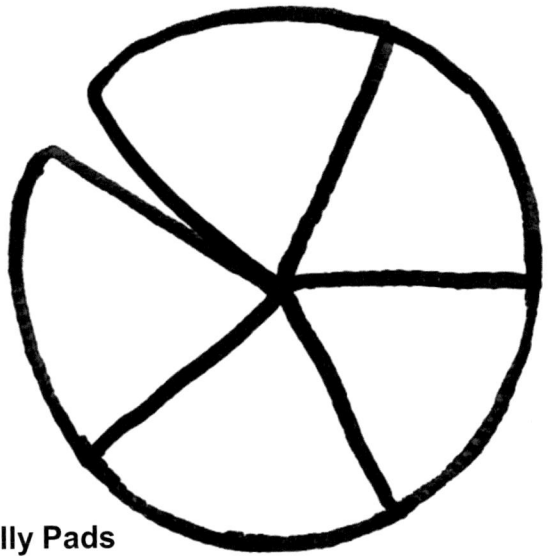

Lilly Pads

Goldfish

Lilly Petal

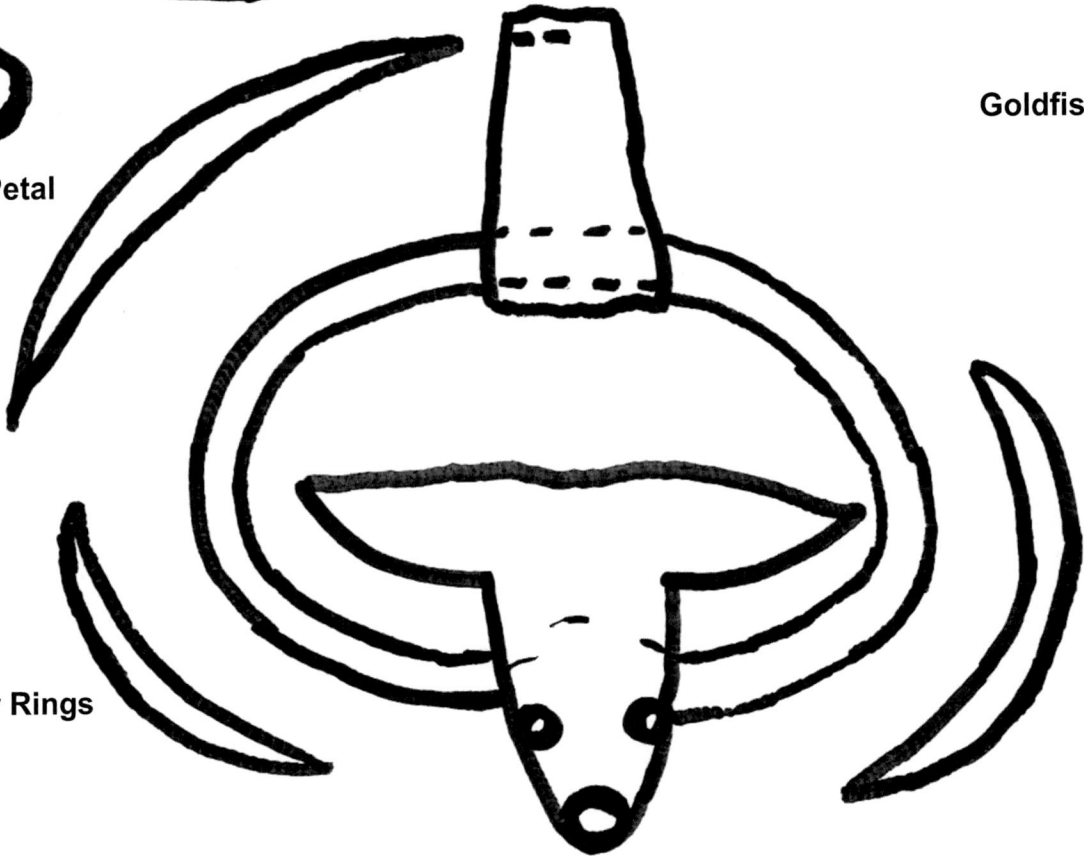

Water Rings

Curiosity, **page 57**

Sampler Floorquilt, Rose Garland, page 64

Rainbow & Sunbonnet Sue, page 64

Alphabet Pattern for Templates

A B C D E F
G H I J K L M
N O P Q R S T
U V W X Y Z

Use a craft knife with caution when
cutting the inner edges of your letters.

A Few Traditional Quilting Patterns

Quilters often enjoy recreating old patterns from the past. Following, are just a few quilting patterns that I have chosen from more than hundreds of old-time favorites. The names of each pattern (there are several) generally reflected the world around the quilters who named the patterns. Aspects of everyday life (early American) led to blocks with names such as *Log Cabin*, *Churn Dash*, and *Wild Goose Chase*. The strong biblical influence of the past is apparent from the large number of blocks with biblical names, such as *Jacob's Ladder*, and *Joseph's Coat*. Throughout the years, each generation of quilters has enjoyed adding their own (pattern) variations to this old and popular art form. Slight variations also complement a few of the 36 patterns that follow, each of which I have penciled onto graph paper. The patterns can easily be drafted by the grid method, using a pencil, ruler, and graph paper. If I can do it—you can do it. Every equal-sized square on your paper may allow for one inch on your floorquilt (see *What's in a Block?* on page 9). You can find a wealth of information on traditional quilting patterns (including much history) by visiting your local bookstore or library, or by searching for traditional patterns online.

"Bear's Paw," one of my favorite quilting block patterns, was easily planned on graph paper. Each square on the graph paper represents one inch on the floorquilt.

"Sawtooth Star"   "Wild Goose Chase" (Variation)   "Jacob's Ladder"

"White House Steps"   "Blossoming Tree"   "Little House"

"Mariner's Compass"   "Ribbon Star"   "Snail-Trail Four-Patch"

"Peony"   "Churn Dash"   "Pinwheel"

Patterns can easily be drafted by the grid method using a pencil, ruler, and graph paper.

"North Wind"

"Four-in-Nine Patch"

"Roman Square"

"Log Cabin"

"LeMayne Star"

"Spool"

"Dutchman's Puzzle"

"Maple Leaf"

"Sail Boat"

"Flower Basket"

"Variable (Ohio) Star"

"Cactus Flower"

After you pencil your pattern, use colored pencils to create a color scheme (see page 10).

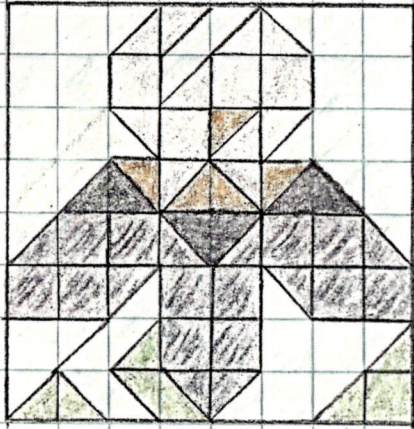
"Iris"

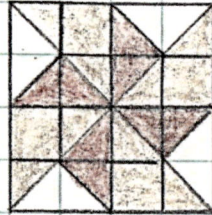
"Double Pinwheel"

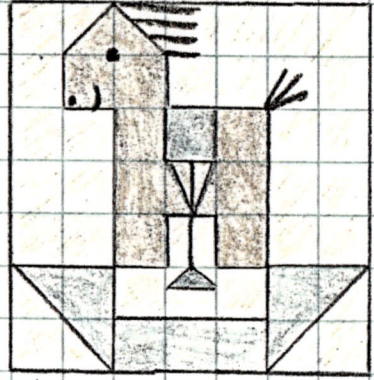
"Hobby Horse"

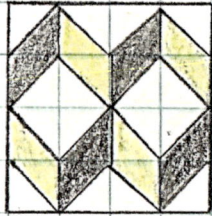
"Ribbons"

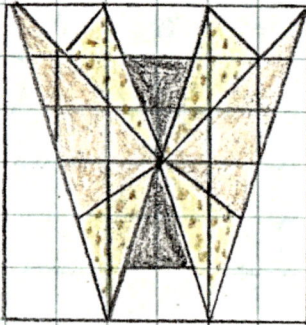
"Butterfly"

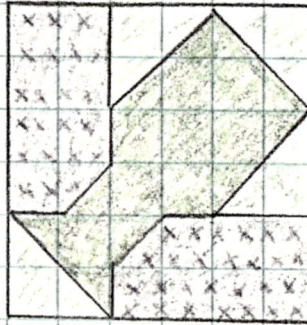
"Goblet"

"The Alfa Plane"

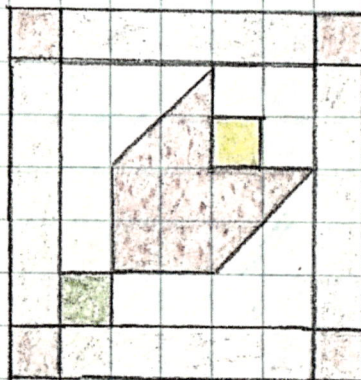
"Pieced Tulip"

"Jewel"

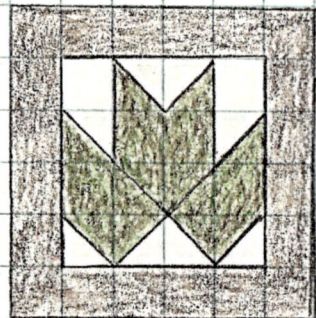
"Tea Leaf"

"Bouquet"

"Wild Rose + Square"

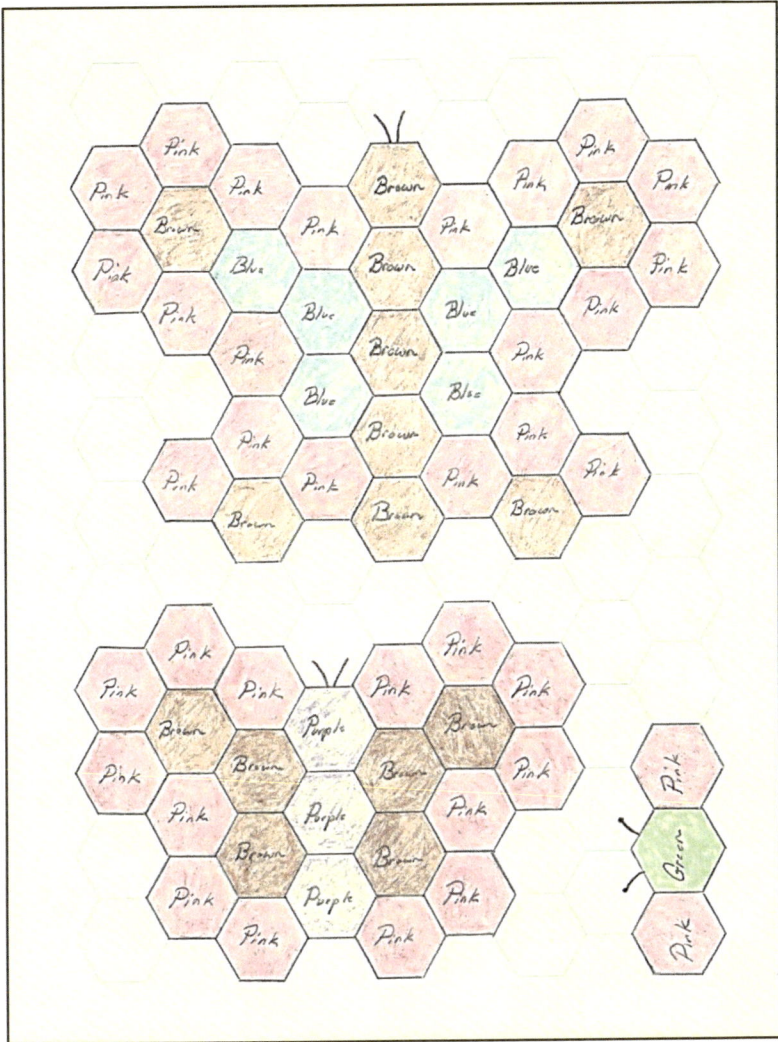

Hexagonal Butterflies

See sources on page 93
for free download of paper,
ruled in hexagons.
For a more precise cut,
hold your plastic template
against your fabric
while you are cutting.
The hexagon template pattern
can be found on page 76.

Fabric: (below) "Roman Glass" by Kaffe Fassett for Westminster Fabrics and Rowan

Glossary & Index
of Floorquilting Terms & Techniques

Appliqué—a design formed with cut pieces of fabric that are applied to the surface of another fabric. (See page 9)

Background Fabric—the foundation material on which appliqués are adhered. (See pages 44 and 52)

Block—a patchwork pattern based on an arrangement of elements that generally form a square. A block may be any size, containing any number of pieces, and can be made up of patchwork, appliqué or a combination of both. (See page 9)

Border—the strips of fabric, plain or pieced, that surround the central portion of a quilt. The border may be decorated using patchwork or appliqué. (See pages 20 and 24)

Border Corner Block—the square that is positioned at each corner of the floorquilt. (See page 24)

Canvas—an extremely heavy-duty plain-woven fabric, used to make furnishings, tents, shoes, and other items for which strength and sturdiness are required. (See pages 16 and 17)

Crazy Patchwork—irregular-shaped pieces of fabric in different sizes and colors, pieced together like a puzzle, in a seemingly crazy manner. (See page 44)

Decoupage—an art form that entails sealing cut-outs (typically paper) to a surface, then covering them with several coats of a clear and protective finish. Fabric decoupage has been a popular art form for many years.

Decoupage Medium—a (non-toxic) water-based glue, sealer, and finish. (See photo on page 12)

Floorcloth—a functional and decorative floor covering, often made from heavy-weight canvas. The treated canvas is usually painted by hand or by stencil before a protective clear finish is applied. (See box on page 19)

Foundation Fabric—a base piece of fabric, which smaller pieces of fabric are applied. (See page 48)

Friendship Quilt—a quilt made as a group project for one member of the group, with each friend making and signing her or his own block. (See page 42)

Hexagonal Patchwork—a geometric design made up of small six-sided blocks (hexagons), which are pieced together on all edges. The sides must be straight, even, and sharp. (See page 48)

Layered Appliqué—the process of applying appliquéd pieces over one another. The pieces are appliquéd to the background fabric, and to each other. (See pages 52 and 57)

Patchwork—designs formed by small pieces of fabric pieced together to form a larger piece. (See page 9)

Pattern—the printed outline for a repeated decorative design on fabric. (See page 9)

Piecing—a process of joining together pieces of fabric to make patchwork. (See page 9)

Sashing—the fabric that separates blocks or squares, framing them to add further interest. (See pages 24, 38, 44, and 64)

Template—a pattern made from durable material, such as vinyl (plastic) or poster board, and used as a guide for drawing pattern pieces onto fabric. This ensures uniformity in the size and shape of each piece. (See page 11)

Happy Floorquilting!

Sources for Tools & Materials

To find the best prices while shopping online, do not forget sites, such as www.ebay.com, www.amazon.com, and www.etsy.com. Just type what you are looking for on the search bar.

Artist canvas (*Fredrix* brand is of high quality) Choose a very heavy-weight, 12 oz. or heavier, 100% cotton duck (see page 16, *What is Canvas?* and page 17).

Cotton duck can be found at many craft and fabric stores.

www.taramaterials.com, www.fredrixartistcanvas.com, and www.hobbylobby.com (for locations)

Art Supply Superstore at www.ebay.com (Type *Fredrix Primed Floorcloth Canvas* on the Search bar)

Gesso primer is available at most art and craft stores. (Not needed if purchasing primed canvas)

www.hobbylobby.com (for addresses) and www.scrapbook.com (enter *gesso* on the search bar)

The decoupage medium, *Mod Podge matte,* can be found at most art, craft, and hobby stores.

www.plaidonline.com or www.hobbylobby.com (for locations) Wal-Mart also carries this product.

Minwax water-based polycrylic (satin, 8 oz.) and clear paste finishing wax are highly recommended.

www.minwax.com, www.lowes.com, and www.homedepot.com Wal-Mart also carries this product.

Rust-Oleum Ultimate water-based polyurethane (satin) is extra durable, and sells in ½ pints (8 oz. cans). It has an ever slight amber hue, and so is not recommended for use over *white* fabrics.

www.rustoleum.com (Type *Ultimate Polyurethane Satin Interior* on the search bar from the homepage) Can also be purchased at www.lowes.com.

Paste wax can be found at most hardware stores in the floor care sections. Lowes and Home Depot **www.lowes.com, www.homedepot.com** or **www.scjohnson.com** (Cannot purchase directly from scjohnson.com)

Template plastic is found at most craft, hobby, and fabric stores, in the quilting sections.

www.hobbylobby.com (locations) or www.joann.com (Type *quilter's plastic template* on the search bar)

Free online graph paper (including hexagonal) www.incompetech.com/graphpaper

Scissors, circle cutters, cutting mats, and rulers, etc. are sold at most craft, hobby, fabric, and department stores in the craft sections. Listed, are a few online stores where they can also be found: www.olfa.com, www.fiskars.com, www.hobbylobby.com (for locations), and www.joann.com

***Saf-T-Bak* rug-backing compound** is generally sold with supplies for rug hooking at craft and hobby stores.

www.amazon.com (Type *Saf-T-Bak rug backing compound* on the search bar for a list of sellers)

A nonskid additive (such as *Skid-Tex* or *H & C SharkGrip*) can be found at some paint stores. www.rustoleum.com (locations) (www.hcconcrete.com–locations–Type *sharkgrip* on the search bar)

Rug pads (nonslip/smooth) are sold at most department and home improvement stores in the rug sections. www.lowes.com Wal-Mart also carries this product.

Fabrics can be found at fabric stores, a few department stores, and hobby and craft stores. When searching for fabric online, type *quilting fabric* on your search engine, and only shop at reputable stores (see pages 12 and 15). Following, are just a few sites that produce and/or sell high-quality fabrics: www.robertkaufman.com, www.kaffefassett.com, www.ttfabrics.com, www.joann.com, and www.hobbylobby.com (for locations)

*"While creating your floorquilt,
take your time,
and enjoy the experience!"*

Converting Inches to Centimeters

Converting inches to centimeters is easy, and following are a few simple ways to do so…

1. After measuring the length in inches with your ruler, simply look at the measurement in centimeters labeled opposite of the measurement in inches.

2. Go to an online converter, such as www.easyunitconverter.com or www.metric-conversions.org (*useful for all unit conversions*). Enter the measurement in *inches*, and what you would like it converted to—*centimeters*. The measurement in centimeters will automatically be displayed.

3. To convert inches to centimeters, **multiply the amount of inches by 2.54**. For example, if you want to convert 24 inches to centimeters, simply multiply 24 by 2.54 to get 60.96 centimeters. That means 24 inches is equal to 60.96 centimeters.

Inches = Centimeters

1................2.54
2................5.08
3................7.62
4................10.16
5................12.7
6................15.24
7................17.78
8................20.32
9................22.86
10.............25.4

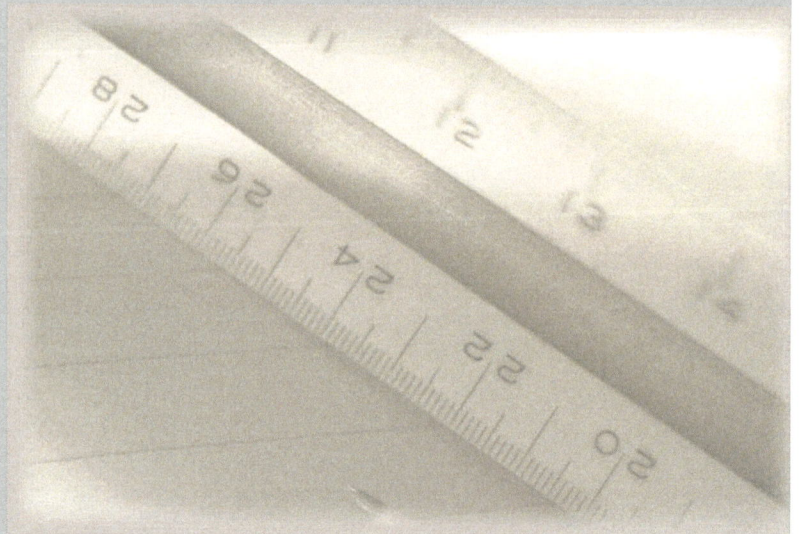

1 yard = 36 inches or 91.44 centimeters

Abbreviations & Symbols

Inches = **in** or **"**   Centimeters = **cm**

About the Author

As an American artist, Carolyn French has always been inspired to create unique and intriguing works of art. Floorquilts, she explains, fit that description. She has fun with floorquilting techniques, and is constantly improving and perfecting this newer and enjoyable craft. Her playful use of fabrics frequently portray whimsical images of animals and fauna in a variety of cheerful, sometimes humorous settings. *"When I am in a fabric store,"* Carolyn relates, *"I love to stroll through the rows and rows of colorful prints. I visualize one vibrant floorquilt after another, and the fun that I will have with all those fabrics, creating a personal and walkable work of art. To think,"* she adds, *"I never have to sew a single stitch!"* Carolyn not only celebrates her own creativity, but also that of others who work with fabrics, and the textile artists who design them.

When she is not floorquilting or searching for colorful fabrics, Carolyn can usually be found with her husband, her two sons, and four indoor cats, who often rouse her creativity. Her workspace is located in the scenic desert southwest, and is surrounded by beauty and inspiration, thus the floorquilt, *Cactus Garden* (above). Her inspiration also comes from her love of gardening, birding, and nature—the underlying concepts for most of her works. Her works—*her vibrant floorquilts can be found beautifying and personalizing homes throughout the country.* Although she enjoys designing and constructing floorquilts for others, it is her hope that whether a person has never sewn, or has years of quilting experience, artist or novice, that he or she find the joy, expressiveness, and sense of accomplishment that comes from making a floorquilt.

21590446R00055

Made in the USA
San Bernardino, CA
27 May 2015